THE GARDEN LOVER'S GUIDE TO

The Netherlands

AND

Belgium

THE GARDEN LOVER'S GUIDE TO

The Netherlands

AND

Belgium

BARBARA ABBS

PRINCETON ARCHITECTURAL PRESS

First published in the United States in 1999 by
Princeton Architectural Press
37 East Seventh Street
New York, NY 10003
212.995.9620

For a catalog of other books published by Princeton Architectural Press,
call toll free 1.800.722.6657 or visit www.papress.com

First published in Great Britain in 1999 by Mitchell Beazley, an imprint of
Octopus Publishing Group Ltd, London

ISBN 1-56898-162-7

For Mitchell Beazley
Executive Art Editor: Vivienne Brar
Executive Editor: Alison Starling
Art Editor: Debbie Myatt
Designer: Terry Hirst
Editor: Selina Mumford
Production: Rachel Staveley
Picture Researcher: Jenny Faithfull
Illustrator: Kevin Robinson
Cartographer: Kevin Jones

For Princeton Architectural Press
Project Coordinator: Mark Lamster
Cover Design: Sara E. Stemen
Special thanks: Eugenia Bell, Jane Garvie, Caroline Green, Clare Jacobson,
Therese Kelly, and Annie Nitschke—Kevin C. Lippert, *publisher*

The publisher also expresses its thanks to all those who collated reference
material for the feature gardens.

All opening and closing hours are correct at the time of publication
but are subject to change. Readers are strongly advised to confirm hours
of operation before visiting the gardens included in this guide.

Half title page: Queekhoven
Title page: Kasteel Hex
Contents page: Han Njio Tuin

Printed in China

Contents

How to use this book

This guide is intended for travellers who wish to visit the most beautiful gardens of the Netherlands and Belgium. The book is divided into five chapters covering the major regions. Each chapter comprises an introductory section with a regional map and a list of the gardens,

followed by entries on each garden. The entries are accompanied by at-a-glance information telling the reader about the garden's defining characteristics and nearby sights of interest. The guide also includes five "feature" gardens, illustrated by three-dimensional plans.

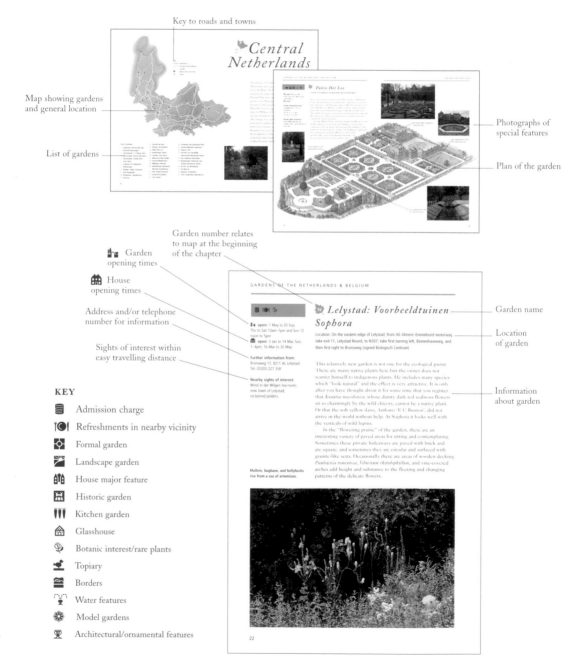

Key to roads and towns

Map showing gardens and general location

List of gardens

Photographs of special features

Plan of the garden

Garden number relates to map at the beginning of the chapter

Garden opening times

House opening times

Address and/or telephone number for information

Sights of interest within easy travelling distance

KEY

Admission charge

Refreshments in nearby vicinity

Formal garden

Landscape garden

House major feature

Historic garden

Kitchen garden

Glasshouse

Botanic interest/rare plants

Topiary

Borders

Water features

Model gardens

Architectural/ornamental features

Garden name

Location of garden

Information about garden

Acknowledgements

A book like this cannot be written without help from a great many people. First and foremost my thanks go to Dorothy Groeneveld, for all her help in so many areas, including translations, hospitality, discoveries, transport, and also to her husband Simon.

I would like to acknowledge the assistance of Chris Riddell and Eurolink Ferries for many pleasant channel crossings and the Hotel Montgomery in Brussels for their hospitality; Pauline Owen at the Belgian Tourist Office has been very helpful as has Madeleine Ralston at the Dutch Tourist Office. My thanks go to all the garden owners who allowed me to look around their gardens, and who frequently provided restoratives as well as information; in particular Piet and Anneke Blanckaert, the Van De Caesbeeks, Dr Anton De Clercq, Claire Hertoghe, Christine and Renaud de Kerchove, Frank von Orshoven, Lette Propre, Patricia van Roosmalen, Roos and John Volckaert, André van Wassenhove in Belgium; in the Netherlands, Madeleine van Bennekom, Ankie Dekker, Ineke Greve, Etta de Haes, Jetty and Jan de la Hayze, Marjan and Dik van Ingen, Lidy Kloeg, Bartle Laverman, Mrs Lenshoek, Han Njio, and Hans Brandsma. A special thank you to Ellen Mayenfeld and Margriet Diepeveen.

In England, Virginia Hinze, John Ramsbotham, Helen and Eric Holder, and Graham Hughes have kindly lent me books and papers. Miranda and Peter Abbs have both done stints of navigation for which I was very grateful. Anyone who knows Christine de Groote's seminal book *Le Guide des Jardins de Belgique*, will realize how much I owe to it. Other authors whose influence I acknowledge with gratitude are Florence Hopper, Erik de Jong, and Simon Schama.

Barbara Abbs, September 1998

The rich colours of late summer in the border at De Heerenhof.

Introduction

"Is there anything except tulips?" was the question I was most frequently asked, when I told people that I was preparing a guide to gardens in the Netherlands and Belgium. Usually quickly followed by even greater surprise that there were any gardens in Belgium at all.

In a way, the Dutch and Belgians have only themselves to blame for the lack of awareness of their gardens beyond their own borders. They do not open them to the public enough. I am very aware that some of the finest gardens have had to be left out of this guide because they are open only to members of specific organizations. It takes some effort for foreigners to find out about these organizations and hence the horticultural richness of both countries remains undervalued. Gardens that open under Open Gardens Schemes in the Netherlands and in Belgium are open only to members of the respective

Massed hydrangeas line steps in the Serres Royale.

organization. For anyone planning to stay in either country for a long period during summer, membership makes some sense (see pages 48 and 97 for information about the open gardens scheme in both countries). However, as readers will realize, as soon as they open this guide, there are many wonderful gardens that will open their gates to foreign travellers.

The Netherlands has a long tradition of garden-making, as well as of horticulture. Early gardens consisted of orchards, lawns for bleaching linen on, and herbs, but very soon there were small designs of box, pleached limes, and mounts. Some of these simple gardens can be seen at the

Nederlands Openlucht Museum Kruidentuin (see p.61). Grander gardens consisted of networks of canals or had quite elaborate hornbeam tunnel-arbours, as at Prinsenhof (see p.18), Paleis Het Loo (see pp.54–7), or Kasteel Amerongen (see p.45), in addition to strong French formal elements. Ever-present water and the flatness of the terrain had a significant effect on garden design, as did the scale of the sites. The fashion for the English landscape style which swept through Europe in the 18th century, resulted in the disappearance of many of the finest Dutch gardens, including Slot Zeist, De Voorst, and Clingendael (see pp.82–3).

Magnificent trees surround the park and lake at Clingendael.

Running parallel to these changing fashions was Dutch horticulture, in particular of course, Tulipomania, which has left its legacy in the thriving Dutch bulb trade and the Keukenhof gardens (see p.86). There are many fine botanic gardens some with collections that date from the early 17th century. Among the cognoscenti, in recent

The elegant orangery at Amerongen.

years, however, the Netherlands has become known for nurseries which are producing subtle and interesting hardy herbaceous perennials and for modern garden design which utilizes ecological knowledge developed from *heemparks* and the pioneering work of J P Thijsse (see p.46). The doyenne of modern garden designers is Mien Ruys (see pp.24–5), whose model gardens span design from 1925 to 1990. Contemporary designers whose work is worth looking out for include Piet Oudolf, Rob Herwig, Elisabeth de Lestrieux, and Arend Jan van der Horst.

The situation in Belgium is somewhat different. There are many fine private gardens in the north, round Antwerp, Bruges and Ghent, and in Limburg, but few of them open with any frequency. In southern Belgium, the French influence was strong and there are several magnificent historic gardens that should not be missed. There are many commercial nurseries, producing trees and shrubs, new cultivars of rose and rhododendron and, of course, the famous Hardy Ghent Azaleas.

The overwhelming impression, however, is of a country where gardens do not matter. Some historic estates have been appallingly commercialized, others split up or neglected. To the outsider it seems as if the concept of an historic garden as a valued work of art has made little impact on the Belgian government. Yet you can drive through the ugliest of towns or villages, turn into a side road and discover private gardens of exquisite design which are beautifully maintained and planted. There are first class designers working in Belgium, including Rene Pechère and Jacques Wirtz, Piet Bekaert, and André Van Wassenhove, whose gardens are worth seeking out. The last two are based in Flanders which has a new and very successful Open Gardens scheme. Details of the special open days are available from your Belgian Tourist Office.

Bold modern planting around the pond in Piet Bekaert's garden near Ghent.

Key to gardens

1 Botanische Vijvertuin Ada Hofman
2 Borg Verhildersum
3 Dehullu Beeldentuin
4 Fraeylemaborg
5 Prinsenhof
6 Hortus Haren
7 Horsthoeve Tuinen
8 Irene Jansen Kijktuinen Kwekerij
9 Jan Boomkamp Tuinen
10 Voorbeeldtuinen Sophora
11 Erve Odinc
12 Menkemaborg
13 Mien Ruys Tuinen
14 Kasteel van Het Nijenhuis
15 Hannie Kamstra
16 Pethitha Tuinen
17 Domies Toen
18 Priona Tuinen
19 Stania-state
20 Tuinen Ton ter Linden
21 Kasteel Twickel
22 Marxveld Historische Tuinen
23 Ommie Hoek and Dirk Bolhuis Tuin
24 Het Warmelo
25 Kasteel Weldam
26 Tuinen van de Westrup

Key

═══ Motorways
─── Principal trunk highways
③ Gardens
● Major towns and cities
• Towns

Northern Netherlands

The Netherlands has been divided, for convenience, into Northern, Central, and Southern. The north comprises the provinces of Flevoland, Friesland, Groningen, Drenthe, and Overijssel.

Flevoland is the newest province of the Netherlands. The reclaimed polder is, like conceptual art, more interesting to read about than to see. There has been considerable tree planting but it is very flat with dead straight roads. There are, however, two gardens that are worth seeing and both use plants native to the Netherlands, but one of them, Voorbeeldtuinen Sophora (see p.22), includes natural-looking species from other parts of the world.

Friesland still has its own language and was separate from the rest of the Netherlands until 1523, when Charles V made it part of the Hapsburg Empire. Much of Friesland is grassland, with many dairy farms and the well-known Friesian cattle. Round the town of Sneek is the Friesian Lake District where the freshwater lakes, dykes, and canals make the area ideal for water sports. You can see the white sails of boats above the banks of

Colourful rhododendrons and azaleas in the 20th-century well garden at Het Warmelo.

13

the dykes from Hannie Kamstra's garden in Offingawier (see pp.26–7). The university town of Leeuwarden, the principal city of Friesland, has some fine buildings and there are a number of estates of interest near Heerenveen.

Groningen, the capital of the province, is a lively university and market town which suffered severe damage during World War II. The Prinsenhof, originally a monastery, then home of the Stadholder of Friesland, has a 17th-century garden (see p.18). Menkemaborg (see p.24) and Borg Verhildersum (see p.17) have attractive gardens outside the moats. Borg is the word signifying a moated manor house.

Symmetrically placed tubs of hostas and daisies create a vista beyond the pond of the Hoek-Bolhuis garden in Groningen.

The poor peaty soil and distant location of the province of Drenthe prevented it from either being heavily developed or intensively farmed until this century. A range of low hills, the *hondsrug*, attracted megalithic settlers, and their tombs, or *hunebeds*, are now tourist attractions. As in the rest of the north, there are many attractive thatched farmhouses with living quarters at one end and housing for animals at the other. Now converted into ordinary dwelling houses, they have become the centrepieces of some of the most exciting gardens in the Netherlands such as that of the artist Ton ter Linden (see pp.30–1) or Pethitha Tuinen near the town of Pesse (see p.27).

Overijssel could be described as *the* garden province. It stretches from the north-east polder and the town of Vollenhove to the German border and is peppered with historic estates, such as Kasteel Twickel (see pp.32–5), Kasteel Weldam (see pp.38–9), and De Wiersse, where the gardens have been laid out over many years and contain a range of historic styles. Here too are the 20th-century gardens of Mien Ruys (see pp.24–5), the doyenne of Dutch garden designers, and Priona Tuinen (see pp.28–9), plus some private gardens. Almost in Germany beyond Oldenzaal are the enchanting Singraven estate and watermill at Denekamp and the excellent arboretum of Poort-Bulten.

Above: Exuberant borders at Hannie Kamstra's garden, Friesland.
Below: Horizontal lines of decking contrast with the verticals of the plants in the Mien Ruys gardens.

open: 1 Apr to 1 Nov, Tue
to Sun and Public Holiday Mon,
10am–5pm

Further information from:
Westeindigerdijk 3,
7778 HG Loozen
Tel: (0524) 562 448

Nearby sights of interest:
Kasteel Coevorden; Gramsbergen:
Streek Museum "Baron van Voerst
van Lynden".

Bold foliage edges a naturally
planted pool in one of Ada
Hofman's water gardens.

1 *Botanische Vijvertuin Ada Hofman*

Location: Take N34 from Zwolle and exit Hardenberg-Oost; on old road from
Hardenberg to Gramsbergen take turn to Radewijk, cross the railway and two
canals, and the gardens are signed

Ada Hofman started this 2.25ha (5½ acre) complex of water
gardens in 1987 and opened it to visitors in 1988. There are over
30 sections, with 50 ponds of every possible type and construction
varying in size from a 420 litre (92 gallon) to a 500,000 litre
(110,000 gallon) capacity. There are three large natural ponds and
adjacent to them enclosed areas containing ponds of prefabricated
shapes, attractively planted and full of such wildlife as grass
snakes, frogs, kingfishers, and over 20 species of butterfly. The
margins are planted, some naturally and others more formally.
Many of the ponds have collections of waterlilies which begin
to flower in early June.

There is a useful key to the plants (everything is labelled
with a letter and number). It has to be said that not all the gardens
are as successful as each other and the overall effect is a little
overwhelming as one garden tends to run into another. If you
are interested in getting ideas, it is a good place to see a range
of materials, different plants, either singly or in combination,
varying designs, and to decide whether the natural pond or
a formal water feature is best for your garden.

As a contrast to the horizontal planes of the lakes
and ponds, there are enormous rock gardens made
with blocks of granite, slate, and, surprisingly, huge
chunks of glass which sparkle and catch the light.

A large informal pond has a sand and pebble
"beach", and a marginal planting of irises and reeds
which changes suddenly to sedums planted in square
blocks. One of the most striking small aquatic gardens
simply contains a raised tank, surrounded by a hedge
of silvery willow and a border of *Artemisia ludoviciana*.
Another has a display of small bowls, planted with
water plants and set on narrow bricks. All around are
well-grown foliage plants, ferns, and ivies.

In the Japanese garden the careful assembly of
gravel, large stones, and evergreens is given a light-
hearted touch with a centrepiece of 13 trimmed trees,
which resemble lollipops with stems of different
heights. Another oriental feature is the Chinese roof
garden, complete with pond, laid out on the roof of
Ada Hofman's private house. In between the ponds,
the observant visitor will find many planting ideas for
the rest of the garden.

Borg Verhildersum

Location: On the N361 21km (13 miles) NW of Groningen; signed

The typical Friesian moated house, approached by a double avenue of lime trees and a wooden bridge, was built in about 1686 although the estate itself dates from the 14th century. A traditional row of pleached stilted limes extends across the front of the low building, where there are also formal box parterres and trained pear trees.

The nearby commune of Leens became responsible for the house in 1953. The curator at that time was Mrs T F Clevering-Meyer and it was she who instigated the formal layout of the garden. A plaque in memory of her can be found on the outside of the pretty restored summerhouse.

A central box parterre with yews at each corner is spoilt by a display of schmaltzy nude statues. There is a raised area at one end where herbaceous plants such as peonies, bergenias, and polygonums are grown. Standard white roses and species roses are mingled with pink ground-cover roses and lavender, creating a very pretty effect. By the perimeter canal there are bold herbaceous plants and box-edged beds of sweet woodruff and borage.

open: All year, Tue to Sun, 10.30am–5pm

Further information from:
Wierde 40, Leens
Tel: (0595) 571 430

Nearby sights of interest:
Groningen; Lauwersmeer.

Traditional pleached limes in the forecourt.

 ## *Dehullu Beeldentuin*

Location: Between Hoogeveen and Emmen; leave A28/E232 Zwolle–Groningen motorway at Knooppunt Hoogeveen and take N37 to Emmen; after about 10km (6¼ miles) take left turn to Geesbrug and Zwinderen; in Zwinderen, take road to Gees where Dehullu-Beelden-in-Gees is well signed

An attractive and well-kept park designed particularly for the display of sculpture.

Broad sweeps of grass, a lake, and small pools are also settings for specialized plant areas: gunneras, conifers, 40 different types of hosta, and a geranium garden with 20 different cultivars and species. Near to the house is a vegetable garden, and, on the other side, a herb garden and a collection of 12 different buddlejas as well as many other trees and shrubs. A fine setting for the varied pieces of contemporary sculpture.

open: 15 May to 30 Sep, Tue to Sun, 1–5pm

Further information from:
Schaapveensweg 16, 7863 Gees
Tel: (0524) 582 141
Fax: (0524) 581 871

Nearby sights of interest:
Emmerdennen Hunebed;
Schimmer-ES Hunebed.

open: All year, daily, sunrise to sunset

open: 1 Mar to 31 Dec;
Tue to Sat and Public Holidays
10am–5pm, Sun 1–5pm

Further information from:
Hoofdweg 30, 9621 AL Slochteren
Tel: (0598) 421 568

Nearby sights of interest:
Museum '40–'45.

 ## *Fraeylemaborg*

Location: 16km (10 miles) E of Groningen; take A7/E32 motorway to Winschoten, then exit 41 Hoogezand; direction Slochteren on N387; signed

The fortified manor house with moat and canal is decorated with white stone pineapples, urns, and the traditional row of pleached limes across the front.

There used to be a formal garden here, probably laid out by Hendrick Piccardt in the late 17th century. Piccardt's father-in-law had owned Fraeylemaborg but had unwisely supported the wrong side in an uprising and been sent to prison. Piccardt, who had spent his youth at the court of Versailles, was rich enough to redeem the estate and renovate the building. There is a rudimentary box parterre but the formal garden has virtually disappeared. It was replaced by a landscape park designed by L P Roodbard in the first half of the 19th century. There are reminders of the past formality, including a row of limes, statuary, and a summerhouse. In the main, the straight avenues became winding paths, the surrounding moat was planted with ferns, and a pool has curved banks and is planted with rushes and ferns.

open: 1 Apr to 15 Oct,
10am to sunset; tea-house: 1 Apr to 15 Oct, Wed to Fri 10am–5pm and Sat and Sun 12 noon to 5pm

Further information from:
Turfsingel 43, Groningen

Nearby sights of interest:
Martinikerk and Martinitoren (tower).

The "Crown" box parterre.

Groningen: Prinsenhof

Location: Near Martinikerk in the centre of Groningen; several entrances, one on Turfsingel canal and another on Kattenhage

The Prinsenhof is a 15th-century building, originally a monastery, which became the Stadholder's residence in 1594. The walled garden in the 17th-century style was reconstructed by E A Canneman from a print which showed a bird's eye view of the city in 1635.

The garden is divided into four. In one section two circular pierced tunnel-arbours, with twelve window apertures and six "doors" in each, are very like the "two-wheeled" garden designed for the Stadholder Maurice in The Hague in about 1620. The remainder of the garden, separated by rose-covered fences and clematis-covered arches, consists of parterres. One parterre has an elaborate crown in box on a ground of white shells, another is planted with roses and lavender, and the third is a herb garden. There are lime trees around the perimeter and a magnificent sundial over the main gate. The tall 15th-century buildings and the sound of the carillon from nearby Martinikerk add to the historical atmosphere of the garden.

6 *Hortus Haren*

Location: 2km (1¼ miles) S of Groningen; Hortus Haren is signed from exit 38, Haren, on A28/E232 Assen to Groningen motorway; well signed in town

open: All year, daily, 9am–5pm

Further information from:
Kerklaan 34, 9751 NN Haren
Tel: (0505) 370 053
(Info-line, Dutch)

Nearby sights of interest:
Havezate Mensinge (manor house), Roden; Kasteel Larwoud; Paterswolde meer.

This is an extensive botanic garden with well-planted modern glasshouses. It would be well worth visiting even without the splendid and very authentic Chinese garden.

There is an arboretum, a pinetum, a rhododendron valley, colour gardens, and bamboo and grass gardens. Naturally, too, there are several rose gardens, an enormous rock garden, and a herb garden. One bed of medicinal herbs is in recognition of the origins of the Hortus. In 1642 the pharmaceutical garden of Henricus Munting was sold to the university and eventually became this garden. It is very attractive, well maintained, and criss-crossed by canals and sheets of water. Plants are well looked after and well labelled.

There is an excellent systematic garden. The tropical glasshouse is very large and includes orchids, tree ferns, and bananas. Local nurserymen display their plants in the Floriade area.

The Chinese garden is a recreation of a prosperous 16th-century official's garden of the Ming Dynasty. Every detail of landscaping and plant selection is said to be authentic, with the Yin and Yang in perfect balance. The garden was still very new and the planting had not yet meshed when this guide was researched, but that was all it needed to be one of the rarest and most satisfying Chinese gardens outside the Orient.

A small temple sits on a rocky mound and other buildings with horizontal lines are built around lakes. You walk across the bridges, through the arches, and by the waterfalls and see a different picture at every step. The area is relatively small but you can never be quite sure that you have seen everything or absorbed the true meaning of the relationship between two pieces of rock.

Allow plenty of time and try to visit the garden when it is not too busy. The Chinese garden was a place of tranquillity and this is not always easy to achieve when it is full of families with excited children.

The temple in the Chinese garden.

Ijhorst: Horsthoeve Tuinen

open: 1 May to 30 Sep, Tue to Sun, 10am–6pm; telephone prior to visit to check opening times

Further information from:
Schotsweg 7, 7951 NP Ijhorst
Tel and fax: (0522) 442 048

Nearby sights of interest:
Staphorst; Vollenhove.

Location: 8km (5 miles) E of Meppel; from A28/E232 take exit 23 to Staphorst, continue through village in direction Ijhorst and Horsthoeve Tuinen are signed

The gardens are laid out around a traditional thatched farmhouse with a magnificent view of the Reest Valley where storks nest.

A fine *berceau* covered with roses and *Cyclanthera pedata*, the climbing cucumber, leads to the house and a romantic orchard. The garden is in two parts, the formal area which consists of box-edged beds of annual and perennial flowers in delightful colours, and a more informal area around what was the former cattle watering place. There is an annual exhibition of bronze sculptures by K Copinga in June, July, and August.

Irene Jansen Kijktuinen Kwekerij

open: Mid-May to mid-Sep, Fri, Sat, and Sun, 10am–5pm; also for four evenings a year between mid-Jul and early Aug, with music and lights

Further information from:
Gasselterweg 41, Gieten
Tel: (0592) 263 310

Nearby sights of interest:
Hunebeds at Borger; Drents Museum, Assen.

Simple modern decking for a seating area by a pool.

Location: 15km (9¼ miles) E of Assen; at Assen-Zuid exit 32 on A28, take N33 direction Veendam and after 15km (9¼ miles) turn right to Gieten; take first left from ring road, into Parallelweg, continue to T-junction and then into Gasselterweg

Irene Jansen is an architect and her show garden has been designed to please but also to inform and educate the many visitors. The garden is laid out in different areas in a variety of styles and in this it resembles the "model gardens" of other designers such as Rob Herwig and Mien Ruys (see pp.24–5). It is a place to come and get ideas, to learn about plant combinations, to see the effects of tiles, stone, and wood, and to understand how different landscape materials can enhance a planting.

Colour-themed herbaceous and mixed borders are a particular feature of the garden. Outside the restaurant is a verandah with tea-tables which overlooks a large pond filled with waterlilies. On one side, the flower borders are made up of warm-toned flowers and on the other, of cool, blue shades. Beyond is an open area, again with colour borders. One foliage and herbaceous border includes annuals to show how their judicious use extends the flowering season until mid-September. Another area is covered with a gravel mulch to illustrate how labour saving this is, effectively suppressing weeds and conserving moisture throughout the season. Every year there are changes, with new borders freshly planted. These give visitors, and especially new gardeners, an example of what to expect – and show how borders develop through the years.

Other striking features include an area paved with blue tiles and embellished with deep blue pots, and a rose pergola with clematis planted around the outside and climbing roses in the interior. In the water garden there are dramatic plantings of *Gunnera manicata* and ligularia. A new water garden is under construction and video programmes are planned to assist gardeners.

Jan Boomkamp Tuinen

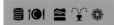

Location: Borne is just N of Hengelo; from A1/E30 Amsterdam–Osnabruck motorway, take exit Hengelo/Borne Westermaat, direction Borne; at second crossroads bear right, the gardens are signed

open: All year, 1 Mar to 15 Nov, Mon to Fri, 9am–6pm, Sat and Sun 10am–5pm

Further information from:
Hesselerweg 9, 7620 AD Borne
Tel: (074) 266 4181
Fax: (074) 266 7995

Nearby sights of interest:
Poort-bulten Arboretum;
Kasteel Singraven; Denekamp
watermoelen.

This rapidly expanding nursery and garden centre has 45 model gardens to view. There are interesting statues round the garden and excellent hard landscaping with many good ideas.

As is the case with many model gardens, there are some striking effects and enlightening plant associations, but also things one would rather not live with. In a "blue and white garden" there is an elegant pergola draped with white and blue wisteria but a rock garden made of chunks of nearby sandstone decorated with slate menhirs.

The large pond in the water garden is surrounded by reeds, watermint, and rushes, and is home to dragonflies and frogs. The English border is based on the ideas of Gertrude Jekyll, and is a traditional mixture of herbaceous plants chosen for colour, habit, and foliage texture. Next to it is the butterfly garden, a double border again, planted with *Buddleja davidii* 'Black Knight' and *B. d.* 'Pink Delight'. The French garden is centred round a spiral yew. In the little garden there is a variegated copper beech, *Fagus sylvatica* 'Rohanii', clipped to a tall cylinder.

There are pot gardens, trough gardens, and even a roof garden, as well as more conventional rose gardens and shade gardens. The divisions between the gardens are as varied as the enclosures themselves with hedges of copper beech, yew, hornbeam, bamboo, and field maple, *Acer campestre.*

A wisteria-covered pergola
at its best.

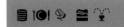

open: 1 May to 20 Sep,
Thu to Sat 10am–5pm and Sun
12 noon to 5pm

Further information from:
Bronsweg 17, 8211 AL Lelystad
Tel: (0320) 227 358

Nearby sights of interest:
Wind in der Wilgen tea-room;
new town of Lelystad;
reclaimed polders.

**Mullein, bugbane, and hollyhocks
rise from a sea of artemisias.**

🍁 10 *Lelystad: Voorbeeldtuinen Sophora*

Location: On the eastern edge of Lelystad; from A6 Almere–Emmeloord motorway, take exit 11, Lelystad Noord, to N307; take first turning left, Binnenhaveweg, and then first right to Bronsweg (signed Biologisch Centrum)

This relatively new garden is not one for the ecological purist. There are many native plants here but the owner does not restrict himself to indigenous plants. He includes many species which "look natural" and the effect is very attractive. It is only after you have thought about it for some time that you register that *Knautia macedonica*, whose dainty dark red scabious flowers sit so charmingly by the wild chicory, cannot be a native plant. Or that the soft yellow daisy, *Anthemis* 'E C Buxton', did not arrive in the world without help. At Sophora it looks well with the verticals of wild lupins.

In the "flowering prairie" of the garden, there are an interesting variety of paved areas for sitting and contemplating. Sometimes these private hideaways are paved with brick and are square, and sometimes they are circular and surfaced with granite-like setts. Occasionally there are areas of wooden decking. *Paulownia tomentosa*, *Viburnum rhytidophyllum*, and vine-covered arches add height and substance to the fleeting and changing patterns of the delicate flowers.

11 *Markelo: Erve Odinc*

Location: About 15km (9¼ miles) E of Deventer; from A1/E30 take exit Markelo, leave Markelo in direction of Rijssen; 4km (2½ miles) out of town, there is a crossroads from Goor to Rijssen, cross straight over but do not take the proper road, take the "parallel way" (which looks like a cycle track) in the direction of Rijssen and the first turning on the right is Seinenweg, and Erve Odinc is down a small path on the right

open: Third weekend in Jun and first two weekends in Jul, 11am–5pm; also Thu between 20 Jun and 15 Jul, 1–5pm; ring to make an appointment for other weekday visits

Further information from:
Seinenweg 2, 7475 TA Markelo
Tel: (0547) 362 843

Nearby sights of interest:
Markelo: known as "fuchsia village"; Huis Verwolde; Rijssen: Pelmoelen "Ter Horst" (windmill).

An enchanting country garden round a traditional thatched farmhouse. Part of the building dates from 1777, some from 1867, and the remainder from 1903. There is a tranquil, timeless quality here with the past constantly in evidence throughout the garden. The house has the authentic row of pleached limes across the front. The compartmentalized garden uses largely local elements – grass, lime trees, box, and flints. Nothing jars.

Beyond the pleached limes there is a lawn partly embraced by a hornbeam hedge with breaks emphasized by domes of yew, or arches allowing views of the surrounding farmland. Borders of foaming catmint, thalictrum, and sweet rocket are contained by low box hedges. A unique summerhouse has been created from a weeping elm.

Topiary columns, like sentinels, add definition and structure to the white garden.

Each façade of the house faces a different garden. In one side garden there is an ancient vine and a box garden. The plants thrive here because this is where all the slaughtering used to be done when the building was a farm and the ground is still rich with blood and bone. The herb garden, an arrangement of box squares, is also a spring bulb garden.

A small tunnel arbour creates a miniature vista. The white garden contains anemones, geraniums, irises, *Artemisia ludoviciana*, cosmos, sweet rocket, and roses. The white is softened by touches of cream, the soft pink of old roses, and palest pink aquilegia. Wisteria forms an arbour over a bench and there are pots of white hydrangea and wild strawberries nearby. It is enclosed with perfect judgement by a high hawthorn hedge.

The vegetable garden is designed around a diamond-shaped bed, with a standard rose as a centrepiece and triangular beds around it.

open: 1 Apr to 1 Oct, daily, 10am–5pm; 2 Oct to 31 Mar, Tue to Sun, as above but closes 4pm; closes January

Further information from:
Tel: (0595) 431 970

The fine façade overlooks one of the most important gardens in the north of the Netherlands.

12 *Menkemaborg*

Location: 22km (13½ miles) NE of Groningen; take N361, N363 to Uithuizen and Menkemaborg is E of town centre

A fine double lime avenue leads up to the imposing moated castle of Menkemaborg. On the right, the formal garden of 1705 is being restored. *Plates-bandes* of double lines of low box hedge planted with small conical yews and carefully spaced flowering plants are in place. Each aquilegia, hosta, iris, lavender, peony, rose, and sedum is planted clear of its neighbours, like a rare specimen. As of course they once were. In the centre there are pretty trellis arbours with cupolas based on an original 18th-century design. Next along this side is the formal rose garden and beyond this is a box parterre.

Behind the castle lies a very formal parterre of triangles of grass, sand, and pebbles, protected by a dense, clipped yew hedge. Continuing through another hedge is a large, thick hornbeam maze. On the other side of the castle beyond the maze, there are *berceaux* of espaliered pear trees and an apple orchard. A formal *potager* is ornamented with a pergola festooned with white and pink climbing roses. These are all small-flowered varieties in white and shades of pink and the effect is charming. In the vegetable beds there are kohl rabi, ferns, thyme, and strawberries.

open: 1 Apr to 31 Oct, Mon to Sat 10am–5pm and Sun 1–5pm

Further information from:
Moerheimstraat 78,
7701 CG Dedemsvaart
Tel: (0523) 614 774

Nearby sights of interest:
Staphorst; Den Berg park; Kwekerij Coen Janssen, Dalfsen.

13 *Mien Ruys Tuinen*

Location: Dedemsvaart is NE of Zwolle; take A28 from Zwolle to Meppel and then exit Nieuwleusen, follow N377 to Nieuwleusen and Dedemsvaart and the gardens are well signed from the centre of the town

The famous Dutch garden designer, Mien Ruys, began her collection of small gardens at her parents' well-known Moerheim nursery 70 years ago. The first two gardens, the Wild Garden and the old Experimental Garden, were laid out in 1925 and 1927. There was a gap of over 25 years, when Mien Ruys was studying architecture and subsequently teaching landscape architecture, before these were joined by the Water Garden (1954) and the Herb Garden (1957). In the 1960s the gardens multiplied, in conjunction with her work as a garden designer.

The garden is still developing, with a new garden of grasses planted in 1993. In 1994, to celebrate Mien Ruys' 90th birthday, 90 different annuals were planted, mixed in borders as well as "bedded out". Although there are always changes in the gardens, the visitor can look at Mien Ruys' work at Dedemsvaart and see her design ideas as they have developed over her lifetime.

In the Experimental Garden one can see the first use of the pebbled concrete slabs that Mien Ruys designed herself, but which are now commonplace. These form a path by a classic English border planted with catmint, delphiniums, geraniums, and golden rod. To the right is the Wild Garden, created among old apple trees around a square pond. The Gardener's Garden is an area for tricky plants. It is designed on different levels so that fussy subjects can have exactly the aspect they like. The Woodland Garden was cleared and planted with rhododendrons and a circle of oxalis punctuated with Solomon's seal in 1987.

Beyond here is an area of smaller model gardens which flow into each other, beginning with perennial borders for shade and sun. The Sunken Garden uses railway sleepers to support different levels. Close by are a pond with reeds, a roof garden, a marsh garden, a yellow garden, and the rose garden proper. A long mixed border is of subtle pinks and purples using weigela, tamarisk, purple-leaved cotinus, and *Rosa* 'Marguerite Hilling'. This is followed by flowering terraces, a garden of grasses, a city garden, a water garden, and a parterre garden.

The Bee Garden was originally designed in 1974 as a rose garden but is now a glorious mélange of shrubs and perennials protected by evergreens, such as *Aucuba japonica* and thuja. In the Herb Garden broad box hedges enclose a central ring of box in which there is a tall iron frame supporting a large silvered glass ball. Planted in small beds, set in paths of narrow bricks, are rue, hyssop, sage, thyme, the red-leaved plantain, and mints.

The silvered glass ball at the heart of the Herb Garden's central box parterre is reputed to ward off evil.

Kasteel van Het Nijenhuis

open: All year, Tue to Sun, 11am–5pm

Further information from:
Hannema-de Stuers Fundatie,
8131 RD Heino/Wijhe
Tel: (0572) 391 434

Nearby sights of interest:
Zwolle: galleries, museums, churches, Milieucentrum Nooter-hof.

The old vegetable garden.

Location: 12km (7½ miles) SE of Zwolle; take N35 in the direction of Almelo and look for signs to Heino; Nijenhuis is 3km (2 miles) from Heino towards Wijhe

There was a manor house here in 1457, but the elegant building today dates from the 17th century when the owner married into the influential Bentinck family and became connected with the court of William of Orange. The two towers were built in the 19th century. The house is now owned by the Hannema-de Stuers foundation. Dirk Hannema was the Director of the Boymans-Beuningen Museum in Rotterdam and his personal collection of paintings, porcelain, and furniture is now housed here. The gardens are used for sculpture exhibitions.

The old vegetable garden has been grassed over and laid out with random squares of grass, yew, lime and beech trees, and striking blocks of salvias and heucheras. The sculptures are displayed on the grass sections. The pieces here and in the rest of the garden are both modern and classical. There is a large, sunken *boulingrin* and a beech *berceau*. The gardens are surrounded by beech woods, where some of the 17th-century avenue layout can be discerned, and an informally shaped canal.

Offingawier: Hannie Kamstra

open: May, Thu 20 and 27, 1–5pm; Jun, every Thu and Sun, and Sat 12 and 19, 1–5pm; Jul, Thu 1, 8, and 15, and Sun 4 and 11, 1–5pm

Further information from:
Griene Dijk 6, 8626 GE
Offingawier
Tel: (0515) 411 138

Nearby sights of interest:
Sneek: Waterpoort, Stadhuis;
Sneeker meer; Heerenveen,
Oranjewoud; Bolsward Stadhuis;
Epema State.

Location: On the eastern side of Sneek, about 20km (12½ miles) S of Leeuwarden; from Sneek take N354, direction Leeuwarden, and in under 1km (¾ mile) turn right to Offingawier and Sneeker meer; before Offingawier take the cycle path, Fietspad, to Sneeker meer (it has a sign indicating no cars, but visitors to the properties may use it), this is Griene Dijk and number 6 is on the right

Hannie Kamstra and her husband, Friesian poet Bartle Laverman, moved to their smallholding at Griene Dijk in 1987 and started the garden the following year. It is still being developed. The rest of their land is used in the traditional way, for farm animals.

The entrance area is shady, planted with lamium, pulmonaria, and other foliage plants. *Hydrangea arborescens* and three standard variegated *Kirengeshoma palmata* immediately catch the eye. This is followed by a tiny courtyard, brimful of hydrangeas, hostas, *Vitis coignetiae*, and *Rosa* 'Veilchenblau'. *R.* 'Paul's Himalayan Musk' grows over the porch. Between the door and the vegetable garden, or *moestuin*, there are more shrub roses and a pergola with different clematis including *Clematis viticella* 'Alba Luxurians' and *C. v.* 'Etoile Violette'. Then comes a square paved garden, dominated by an old apple tree draped with the climbing rose, *R.* 'Lykkefund'. Beyond this is a dramatic red border with, among other plants, *Heuchera* 'Palace Purple', the rusty pink polygonum *Persicaria amplexicaulis*, and clipped box balls. There are white and yellow borders, two orchards, and a tiny wood underplanted with *stinzenflora*.

The second half of the garden is still being developed. Wild roses and elder flourish in the boundary hedges. There is a new lake and planting has just begun on the far side. A bank of bright yellow and gold daylilies, loosestrife, helenium, ligularia, and inula draws you to the far end of the garden.

On your return you notice the sitting area, a circle full of flowers surrounded by rugosa roses, and another ring of roses on a pergola where climbing roses, including *Rosa* 'New Dawn', enclose a circular area which captures the scent of roses within it.

 ## *Pesse: Pethitha Tuinen*

Location: 6km (3¾ miles) N of Hoogeveen on A28/E232; take exit 28, Ruinen, and then direction Pesse, continue for 1.5km (1 mile) through Pesse, then turn right in direction of Gysselte, then under motorway and turn right; well signed

open: 25 May to 25 Sep, Tue to Sun, 1–5pm

Further information from:
Molenhoek 10, 7933 TG Pesse
Tel: (0528) 241 607

Nearby sights of interest:
Tuinen Ton ter Linden
(see pp.30–1).

This is a garden of differently coloured garden "rooms". Hans Brandsma began it in 1988 and it has expanded year by year as the various compartments have been developed. The colour combinations are all wonderfully rich and exciting.

The yellow garden has a background of golden hops and 3m (10ft) high bronze and yellow *Helianthus* 'Red Velvet' and *H.* 'Lemon Moon' towering over a delicious mixture of lime-green *Nicotiana langsdorfii*, *Aconitum* 'Ivorine', and the annual *Eschscholzia* 'Milky White'.

Antirrhinums in the dusky red garden.

A glowing, deep-toned garden of dusky reds includes *Atriplex hortensis* var. *rubra*, *Berberis thunbergii atropurpurea*, an unusual umbellifer, *Cryptotaenia japonica atropurpurea*, ruby chard, and the brilliant scarlet dahlia, 'Bishop of Llandaff'. Near the house, on one side of the central lawn, is a mauve border with veronicas, phlox, and bergamots. There is a peaceful view of the open fields. On the other side of the lawn is a border of resonant blues, with echiums, *Clematis integrifolia*, *Salvia patens*, and bold clumps of the coarse, glaucous grass, *Leymus arenarius*.

An archway leads to more rooms, including late summer gardens of sedums, phloxes, and Michaelmas daisies.

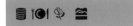

open: At all times

Further information from:
Hoofdstraat 76, 9968 AG
Pieterburen
Tel: (0595) 528 636

Nearby sights of interest:
Koffie-en Winkel Museum.

The old summerhouse.

Pieterburen: Domies Toen

Location: N of Groningen near coast; take N631 for about 16km (10 miles),
then at crossroads take road to Eenrum and Pieterburen; the garden adjoins
Dutch Reformed Church

The Domies Toen or Vicar's Garden has been in existence in
Pieterburen for over 300 years. It is adjacent to the churchyard
and the 15th-century church towers over it. There are varying
levels and the paths wander from one area to another in an
uncontrived way. This very agreeable garden has a number of
miniature landscapes within it. Among them are a lake with native
water plants and marsh vegetation like yellow flag
irises and purple loosestrife; meadowland dotted
with fritillaries, lady's smock, and ox-eye daisies;
wayside plants which are found on the shoulders
of roads and dykes, such as yellow salsify and
ramping fumitory; and the fast disappearing flowers
of cornfields, including cornflowers, poppies, and
corn marigolds. Overlooking the meadows is the
former vicar's pretty summerhouse.

There are several semi-woodland patches
planted with shade-loving plants and *stinzenflora*.
A fascinating feature in the garden is the Aeolus
windharp, a copy of a 19th-century instrument
made by a local harp builder. To hear it suddenly
sound as the wind blows is truly magical.

open: 30 Apr to 30 Sep, Tue to
Sat 12 noon to 5pm and Sun
2–6pm

Further information from:
Schuineslootweg 13, 7777 RE
Schuinesloot, bij Slagharen
Tel: (0523) 681 734

Nearby sights of interest:
Slagharen Pony Park;
Kasteel Coevarden.

Priona Tuinen

Location: About 35km (21¾ miles) NE of Zwolle; Slagharen is on the N377 between
Dedemsvaart and Coevarden; in Slagharen take the road to Hollandscheveld and
then turn right after 2km (1¼ miles) to Schuinesloot (this is Schuineslootweg)

Holland is full of gradations of the *heemtuin*, from the absolutely
pure, where only plants native to Holland are allowed, to the
gardens of Ton ter Linden (see pp.30–1), where a flowering
meadow effect is achieved in a highly sophisticated way. At
Priona, the balance falls distinctly towards the natural. Visitors
have been known to complain that there are only weeds to be
seen, but most people prefer to call them wildflowers and marvel
at the range, colour, and the artistry with which they are combined.

Many of the plants at Priona have been studied growing in
their natural habitats throughout Europe. When the same species
have been planted in the gardens, as far as possible, they have
been given the same soil and aspect. Through an arch covered

with *Rosa* 'New Dawn' is Hemelsleuteltuin, a dank corner where Welsh poppies, thalictrum, and ferns flourish, followed by *Holodiscus discolor* and *Rodgersia pinnata* late in the season.

Round the next corner is Hochstaudenfleur, which has more sun and better soil. The majority of flowers are from central Europe, such as lunaria, polemonium, and trollius. However, they have been augmented by American and Asian plants that like the same conditions. Then a narrow path cuts through part of the naturally regenerating wood which surrounds the garden and emerges in the Vlindertuin. Here dozens of spears of *Verbascum thapsus* rise from a quilt of catmint, origanum, lavender, sweet rocket, and daisies like Roman legions on the march.

A pot garden adjoins the area of the shop, tea-house, and terrace which overlooks the pond, alive with green frogs. The water is covered with yellow *Nuphar lutea*, frogbit, *Hydrocharis morsus-ranae*, and water soldier, *Stratiotes aloides*. Delicate white waterlily moths flutter around. There are also newts and toads and, on the pond margin, reeds, grasses, irises, mimulus, and white balsam. Still to come is the Great Border, with soft apricot poppies, geraniums, *Rhayzya orientalis*, and a cool *Stachys byzantina*.

Parallel to the Great Border, and separated from it by a ribbon of trees and shrubs, is the All American Garden, with a willow-leaved pear (*Pyrus salicifolia*), *Gillenia trifoliata*, many grasses, *Coreopsis verticillata*, and *Ribes speciosa*. The herb garden is full of herbs from southern Europe that grow naturally together. The vegetable garden has an unexpected jumble of cabbage, rhubarb, fruit, currants, mullein, and the grass *Carex greyi*.

Weeds, wildflowers, or just beauty? This delicate flowery meadow effect, with poppies and corn cockle, is characteristic of Priona gardens.

⬛⬛🏆

open: At all times

Further information from:
Rengersweg 98, Oenkerk
Tel: (0582) 562 811

Nearby sights of interest:
Another example of Roodbard's landscaping at Vijversberg, Zwartewegsend 2, Rijpekerk (Ryptsjerk), 6km (3¾ miles) E of Leeuwarden on the N355 to Groningen.

 ## *Stania-state*

Location: Oenkerk (Oentsjerk) is 10km (6¼ miles) NE of Leeuwarden; take N355 road to Groningen and after 6km (3¾ miles) turn left onto N361 to Oenkerk; the village is 5km (3 miles) and Stania-state is on the right past the VVV on the left

This well-designed garden, by the Dutch landscape architect, L P Roodbard, was created between 1823 and 1843. The trees are now imposingly mature with inspiring circles of oaks, and a magnificent weeping beech on a mound that rises from one of the curving lakes. A rustic bridge links the islands across the lake to the "mainland", and there is also a tiny grotto nearby. A straight axial path leads to a circle of oaks and an open lawn with a central statue. A fine series of 18th-century statues survey another large glade.

It is easy to imagine that one is in a landscape park in England in Stania-state, so skilfully have the contours and mounds been constructed. One has to step back into the pancake-flat, dyke-crossed countryside outside the gate to fully appreciate Roodbard's expertise. Refreshments are served at the weekend.

open: 30 Apr to 1 Oct, Tue to Sun, 10am–5pm

Further information from:
Achterma 20, 7963 PM Ruinen
Tel: (0522) 472 655

Nearby sights of interest:
Pethitha Tuinen (see p.27).

A typical Ton ter Linden planting.

Tuinen Ton ter Linden

Location: NE of Meppel; from Groningen, A28/E232 take exit 28 Pesse/Ruinen; from Meppel, A28, then A32 Leeuwarden, exit 3 Meppel-Noord then N375 to Ruinen; well signed

The spring border in late May is a cloud of aquilegias, Shirley poppies, thalictrum, geraniums, and alliums. Small flowers in shades of mauve shimmer in the breeze. But flaming among this well-bred bunch are huge, incandescent orange oriental poppies. It is a typical piece of Ton ter Linden's planting. Broad grass walks are lined with straight dark green yew hedges which constantly entice and conceal. Hidden behind the yew next to the spring border is the great sunny border designed for high summer. Here the giant plume poppy, *Macleaya cordata*, and spikes of *Veronicastrum virginicum* contrast with the firm satiny flowers of lilies, the flat golden heads of achillea, foamy *Alchemilla mollis*, and cool silvery *Artemisia ludoviciana*. Intense colour comes from *Lychnis chalcedonica* and clumps of mauve, cherry, and vermilion phlox.

The majority of the planting is of hardy herbaceous plants. There are few exotics and the influence of J P Thijsse (see p.65) is

noticeable in the use of indigenous plants throughout the garden. There are drifts of *Persicaria bistorta* 'Superba' sprinkled with ragged robin, swathes of yellow deadnettle, glistening buttercups, and a thickly planted patch of sweet rocket in palest mauves and white mixed with dark *Viola cornuta*. The delicacy of the wildflowers adds a magical shimmer to the garden.

Sumptuous oriental poppies and majestic irises are planted with arching grasses and clumps of daisy flowers.

Other areas include an old rose border; a square set with spherical acacias surrounded by hornbeam hedges; a garden of grasses round a square pool which overlooks surrounding farmland; an autumn garden with sedums and a rose pergola planted with species and old roses. There is a blue and lilac garden, a walled garden, a herb garden, and a woodland garden where daylilies, species foxgloves, astrantia, alchemilla, and hostas prosper under the trees in the shade.

A wild pond with tiny green frogs contrasts with a more formal pond garden. A ginkgo tree stands sentinel over a square pond edged with decking on which sit asymmetrically placed pots. This geometry is softened by a planting of grasses, hostas, and peltiphyllum. In a damp corner, shaded by alders, water bubbles through a stone and a pergola surrounds climbing hydrangeas underplanted with spring bulbs, which include fritillaries, white bluebells, and ornithogalums. In the shrub garden, purple heuchera, sage, tulips, and alliums are mixed with ground-cover roses. Under a group of viburnums there are hostas, sombre *Geranium phaeum*, and fluffy mauve thalictrum.

Round the garden there are works of art which change from year to year. Unhappily, here, as elsewhere, the artworks do not compare with the planting.

Kasteel Twickel

open: Mid-May to mid-Oct, Mon and Fri, 11am–5pm; last admission 3.30pm; tea-house in orangery: 1–4.30pm

Further information from: Stichting Twickel, Postbus 2, 7490 AA Delden Tel: (0743) 761 212

Nearby sights of interest: Delden: De Noordmolen (oil mill); Jan Boomkamp Tuinen (see p.21); Kasteel Weldam (see pp.38–9).

Location: 6km (3¾ miles) W of Hengelo and NW of Enschede; from A1/E30 from Deventer, take A35 direction Hengelo Zuid/Enschede, then exit 28 Delden to N346; by water tower, follow signs to Delden/Bornerbroek then follow signs left to Twickel

If the name Twickel sounds familiar it is probably because of *Lavandula* 'Twickel Purple', which was given an award of merit in 1961 and is still popular. Twickel has one of the prettiest castle gardens in the Netherlands. It has had a long and chequered history but its charm today must surely be the legacy of the last owners, Baron Rodolphe van Heeckeren and his wife, the Baroness van Heeckeren, an enthusiastic and knowledgeable gardener who worked in the garden until her death at the age of 86 in 1975. The Baroness was born Gravin van Aldenburg Bentinck and grew up first at Middachten (see p.60) in Gelderland and later at Kasteel Zuylestein, both estates with fine gardens. It was she who first discovered the deep-purple lavender.

The castle rises from the waterlily covered moat.

The famous topiary parterre lies between the orangery and the moat.

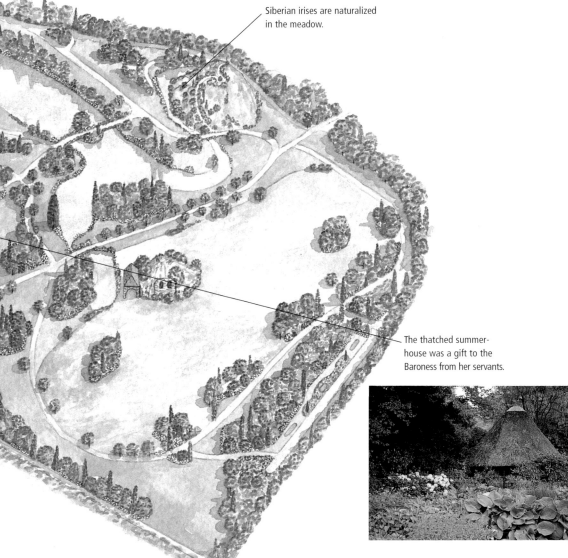

Siberian irises are naturalized in the meadow.

The thatched summerhouse was a gift to the Baroness from her servants.

The area known as the "Rockery" in spring.

The orangery and the parterre, which dates from 1906.

A plan exists showing the 17th-century garden. The castle and the *cour d'honneur* are surrounded by a moat and the Renaissance garden is laid out around it, inside a perfectly square canal. There are trees, a knot garden, a vegetable garden, and an orchard with *berceaux*, and a grass area that was used for bleaching linen. In about 1700, Baroque flourishes were added. The canal was enlarged to enclose an oblong garden and designs for elaborate parterres and shrubberies were submitted by Daniel Marot, although it is probable that these were never executed. At the end of the century a plan by Hartmeyer shows the canal widened and with curving banks, giving a lake-like appearance. This was part of an Anglo-Chinese garden. All the formal parterres have gone and have been replaced by sinuous paths, woodland, streams, and inlets. Beyond the water was a deer park, a mount, and an icehouse.

Many famous Dutch landscape designers worked on these gardens, including Johan Georg Michael and three generations of the Zocher family. J D Zocher the younger worked here between 1830 and 1835 and simplified the gardens, basing his design on the landscape principles of Capability Brown. C E A Petzold, a German landscape designer who did a considerable amount of work in the Netherlands, added exotic trees and

shrubs and expanded the mirror pond behind the orangery. Towards the end of the 19th century, however, the garden round the house again became more formal. In 1906 parterres in front of the orangery were designed by Edouard André's assistant, Hugo Poortman who was living and working at nearby Kasteel Weldam (see pp.38–9). The famous topiary peacocks, squirrels, and other animals appeared and a rose garden was laid out. This is now grassed over. The orangery was restored in 1993 and looks splendid once again. Palms, fuchsias, orange trees, oleanders and olives, *Aloysia triphylla*, pomegranates, agaves, and other tender plants stand outside it during the summer. The parterres are full of tulips in spring and the formal topiary garden, with the crisply trimmed animals and birds, is still in excellent condition.

The Baroness made a rock garden in 1932 behind the orangery and the formal garden. This area, the only part of the garden where she could grow what she wanted to, was too shady and the soil too acid for most rock plants but it is still referred to as the rockery. There is a lawn and beds of rhododendrons, azaleas, and *Stewartia pseudocamellia* underplanted with many other woodland plants, including trilliums and smilacina. Huge oak trees shade a thatched summerhouse which was presented to the Baroness on her 80th birthday. Nearby are gates leading to the lake and the rock garden. Here curving flowerbeds hummocky with brightly coloured rock roses, mossy saxifrage, and smooth boulders left over from the ice age are cut out of the lawns.

The 18th-century mount still exists. It can be ascended and affords a pleasant view over a lake and a meadow of Siberian irises.

Looking down from the 18th-century mount.

The Baroness's "Rockery" was too shady for alpine plants, but makes a fine woodland garden.

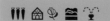

open: All year, daily, sunrise to sunset

Further information from:
Bisschopstraat 22, Vollenhove
Tel: (0527) 249 222

Nearby sights of interest:
Onze Lieve Vrouwekerke;
Blokzijl; Giethoorn.

The Baroque parterre.

22 *Vollenhove: Marxveld Historische Tuinen*

Location: Vollenhove is between Meppel and Emmeloord, NW of Zwolle on the Noord-Oost polder; the gardens are adjacent to the Onze Lieve Vrouwekerke (church) behind Bisschopstraat

These gardens in four different historic styles were laid out in 1988. The periods chosen reflect important moments in the history of Vollenhove, a harbour town dating from the 11th century.

The Medieval garden represents the period from the Middle Ages to 1500. It is the simplest of cloisters round a well and a mulberry tree. The Renaissance garden, reflecting the garden style of between 1500 and 1600, is divided into simple shapes. Four yew-hedged rectangles with pleached limes are filled with herbs, meadow flowers, and more colourful but perhaps less authentic cultivated flowers.

The Baroque garden, 1600 to 1760, has a central fountain and pool. The outer perimeter, a double hedge of box enclosing a narrow strip of flowers, is bright with daylilies, irises, peonies, and tradescantia. The Landscape garden does not have the correct scale for an 18th-century landscape park, but the rest of the garden is extremely pleasant.

---

open: May to Oct, daily, 10am–5pm

Further information from:
Oostervalge 25, 9989 EJ Warffum
Tel: (0595) 422 487
(Dutch spoken only)

Nearby sights of interest:
Warffum: 14th-century church, "Het Hoogeland" open lucht museum (open-air museum).

23 *Warffum: Ommie Hoek and Dirk Bolhuis Tuin*

Location: About 25km (15½ miles) N of Groningen via Winsum to Uithuizen; coming from Groningen, the garden is on the left after built-up area of Warffum

The green-fingered owners of this garden work in it all day every day and it shows. It is one of the most delightful and immaculate small gardens in Holland.

Drive slowly along the road and you will easily distinguish number 25. On one side of the path there is a pink border, with *Salvia sclarea*, *Lavatera* 'Barnsley', *L. rosea*, and *Rosa* 'The Fairy', plus a dark-leaved phlox, a mauve-pink clematis, astrantia, and lilies in pots. The house itself is smothered with the vines of *Actinidia chinensis*, *Clematis* 'Jackmanii', and pink hydrangeas. Across the path is an array of tender and unusual plants in pots.

There are formal vistas and box-edged beds full of pale, softly coloured flowers. Symmetry plays an important part in the garden: two pots of felicia stand by the sides of the path to the back garden. The move from one hedged area to another through a clematis-covered arch is further emphasized by a pair of willow-leaved pears and two clumps of ornamental grass. Beyond a hedge of silvery willow is the fruit garden where there are old local varieties of apples and pears. A small greenhouse is packed with three different vines, species begonias, orchids, and Stag's horn ferns (*Platycerium bifurcatum*) of a luxuriance not usually seen outside a rainforest. And there is still more to see in this small garden, for there is a rock garden and a pond with waterlilies and a shoal of black and gold fish.

Het Warmelo

Location: About 20km (12½ miles) SW of Hengelo, 8km (5 miles) S of Goor; signed on N346 Hengelo to Zutphen

The house and gardens at Warmelo were restored in the 1920s by the Baroness Creutz with the professional help of designer Hugo Poortman, a pupil of Edouard André, who had also worked at Kasteel Twickel (see pp.32–5) and Kasteel Weldam (see pp.38–9).

The garden is a complex of gardens dating from different periods, including an 18th-century landscape garden, a French formal garden, and a pinetum which dates from the Victorian age.

The marked route leads around the outside of the garden and gradually spirals into the centre. On the right as you enter is the 20th-century well garden, with two rills, rhododendrons, and azaleas. Yew hedges enclose the garden and there is a collection of standard fuchsias and lantanas. Then follows a marsh garden from where a lane of birches leads to a woodland glade, with a *Davidia involucrata* and other exotic trees.

The English landscape garden follows. Halfway round there is a sudden splendid view of the house across a lake, a canal, and the moat. Another detour leads to a small mount, planted with azaleas. Then there is the pinetum. A lawn with serpentine edges is enclosed by majestic conifers which create a natural nave. Groups of large prostrate junipers make a fine contrast. At the end of the lawn there are azalea borders.

From this Victorian grandeur, there is another sudden change of style as one enters first the French star garden and then the French Rococo garden with a stone *bassin* accompanied by four symmetrically placed spiral-clipped box trees. This is an exquisite formal garden and forms another of the delightful

open: 30 Apr to 15 Oct, Tue and Thu, 1.30–5pm; May to Jun, Sun and Public Holidays, 10am–5pm; Jul to Oct, first Sun of month, 10am–5pm

Further information from:
7478 RV Diepenheim
Tel: (0547) 351 280
Fax: (0547) 352 547

Nearby sights of interest:
De Wiersse; Kasteel Weldam (see pp.38–9); Huis Verwolde; "Den Haller" (cornmill), Diepenheim.

Exquisite French Rococo formality.

contrasts which make Warmelo so special. The marked way continues across the lawn in front of the house, between the canal and the moat, to the rose garden and the fuchsia garden. These gardens are enclosed by tall hedges and laid out in formal beds. The visit continues via the menagerie and finishes at the forecourt planted with ancient mulberries.

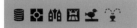

open: All year, Mon to Fri, 9am–4pm

Further information from:
Diepenheimseweg 114,
7475 MN Markelo
Tel: (0547) 272 647
Fax: (0547) 260 402

Nearby sights of interest:
Kasteel Twickel (see pp.32–5); Markelo "fuchsia village"; "Den Haller" (cornmill), Diepenheim.

The *parterre de broderie* and hornbeam tunnel in autumn.

25 *Kasteel Weldam*

Location: Near Goor about 15km (9¼ miles) W of Hengelo; from N346 Hengelo to Zutphen take the second road to the left to Diepenheim, after the N347 turning to Haaksbergen; the turning is on a bend, and is only marked by "P" for parking

The garden at Weldam is a fine re-creation of a 17th-century garden, in sympathy with the mid-17th-century house which it surrounds. It was laid out by Hugo Poortman in 1886 from a design by Edouard André. Poortman was André's pupil and, later, became his office manager. Mature trees that had been planted in the 19th century were retained and the garden was designed around a series of axes that follow the lines of the moat.

A short avenue leads to the entrance court and on the left-hand-side of the drive, where there used to be one of two symmetrical *parterres de compartiment*, there is a sunken garden, where orange trees in traditional *caisses de Versailles* are set out along the raised walk. On the far side is what seems to be a huge hedge. This reveals itself to be a magnificently proportioned hornbeam tunnel over 100m (328ft) long. The rear wall of one of the buildings which forms the entrance court is planted with trained fruit trees and tender climbers. There is a wonderfully intricate box *parterre de broderie* in the long rectangle between here and the tunnel, with a grass parterre in the centre and, to counteract the very horizontal effect, large pyramids of box and yew.

The splendid thuja maze has now reached a height that makes it quite daunting. However, there is a central viewing platform to assist the baffled visitor. Domed yews march all around the sunken lawns, or *boulingrins*, behind the castle and around another piece of

broderie, a half moon of yew scrolls whose shapes can only be appreciated from the viewing platform in the maze. The axis through the house from the forecourt continues through the half moon, across a canal enlarged to a formal pool, and out into the surrounding parkland.

Returning by the other side of the house, there is a bank of rhododendrons and a parallel vista where specimen trees have been retained. Two lawns surrounded by flowering shrubs balance the *parterre de broderie* on the other side. There is also a formal rose garden.

 # *Tuinen van de Westrup*

Location: 15km (9¼ miles) N and slightly W of Emmen; take N34 Emmen Groningen and take turn to Westdorp after 15km (9¼ miles); signed from the centre of the village

open: Group bookings only, telephone to make an appointment

Further information from:
Brink 9, Westdorp (gem Borger)
Tel: (0599) 235 402

Nearby sights of interest:
Hunebeds, Borger; Ter Apel.

Skilful use has been made of this long narrow site parallel to a country lane. It extends on both sides of the attractive farmhouse, the last remaining building of the de Westrup castle estate. Paths wind between tall, uncontrived borders of heuchera, purple plantain, verbascums, foxgloves, veronicas, teasles, and *Allium sphaerocephalum*: plants with dramatic form and distinctive texture.

Informal borders are ideal in this rural setting.

The garden was started ten years ago. The shrubs and trees are still small but the herbaceous plants are luxuriant. Much use is made of bamboos, grasses, and teasles. There are some exciting plant combinations: brilliant purple, large-flowered *Malva mauritiana*, the mauvey-crimson of *Echinacea purpurea*, *Eschscholzia* 'Milky White' which is actually palest yellow, and *Nicandra physalodes*. White verbascum grows out of a sea of the blue grass, *Leymus arenarius*.

On the south-west boundary there are conifers and evergreens such as box, holly, and berberis with *Lonicera japonica* 'Aureo-reticulata' rambling over them. Plants seed themselves and only if they are absolutely out of place are they weeded out.

Pieces of sculpture are displayed around the garden, and there are more sculpture and graphics on show in a converted barn.

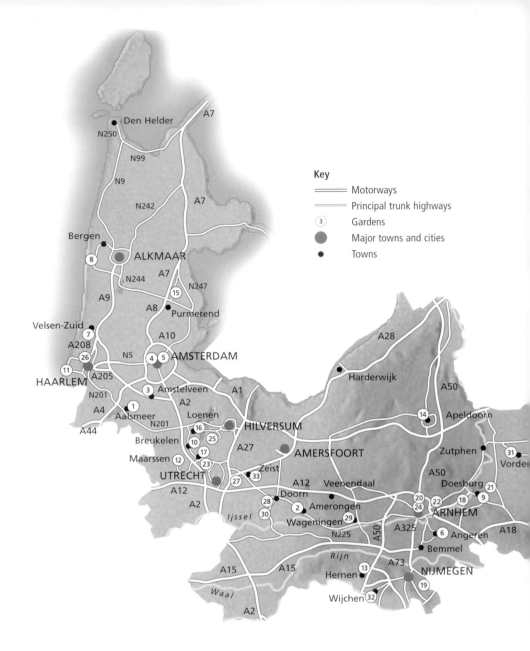

Key

═══ Motorways
─── Principal trunk highways
③ Gardens
● Major towns and cities
• Towns

Key to gardens

1 Historische Tuin, Aalsmeer	13 De Brinkhof	24 Sonsbeek and Zypendaal Parks
2 Kasteel Amerongen	14 Paleis Het Loo	25 Kasteel-Museum Sypesteyn
3 J P Thijsse Park	15 Koelemeijer Tuinen	26 Thijsse's Hof
4 Hortus Botanicus, Amsterdam	16 Terra Nova	27 Fort Hoofddijk Universiteit
5 Vondel Park and others	17 May Hobijn	Botanische Tuinen
6 De Hagenhof	18 Kasteel Middachten	28 Von Gimborn Arboretum
7 Beeckestijn	19 Millinger Theetuin	29 Belmonte and Driejen
8 Sijtje Stuurman	20 Nederlands Openlucht	Botanische Tuinen
9 Huis Bingerden	Museum Kruidentuin	30 De Hof van Walenburg
10 Queekhoven	21 Kwekerij Piet Oudolf	31 De Wiersse
11 Elswout	22 Kasteel Rosendael	32 Arnoldshof
12 Kasteel De Haar	23 Slot Zuylen	33 Dieptetuin Valkenbosch

Central Netherlands

The province of Gelderland is the largest in the Netherlands and is geographically divided by three rivers, the Rhine, the Maas, and the Ijssel. The Rhine separates the rough sandy heath of the Hoge Veluwe National Park from more fertile country south of the province near Nijmegen. While the Hoge Veluwe is the location of some great hunting estates, including that of Paleis Het Loo (see pp.54–7), originally a hunting lodge for William of Orange, horticulture, arable farming, and orchards are found around Nijmegen and naturally enough, it is excellent gardening country with many good private gardens (see pages 32 and 70). Arnhem is particularly rich in historic gardens including Kasteel Rosendael (see pp.62–3) and Zypendaal Park (see p.64), the headquarters of the historic houses trust for Gelderland which looks after important properties such as Huis Verwolde and De Voorst. Open by appointment and under the Netherlands Open Gardens scheme is the finely planted garden of Mrs Lidy Kloeg at 6 Braamweg, Arnhem.

While rich nobles acquired country estates in Gelderland, wealthy merchants from

Hydrangeas flourish by the waterside at Terra Nova on the Loosedrechtse.

41

Amsterdam built themselves country houses around the River Vecht in the province of Utrecht. Several of the buildings remain, such as Goudesteyn, now Maarssen Town Hall, Gunterstein, Nijenrode and Over-Holland, but the once-elaborate 17th-century gardens with their canals and parterres have long gone. The Gooiland area of woodland and water north of Utrecht and the Vecht is beautiful and surprisingly peaceful (see Terra Nova on pages 58 and 59) in spite of the pressures of development.

Noord-Holland and Utrecht today are part of the most densely populated area of the Netherlands known as Randstad or "Ring city" – two loops of densely built-up land which include Amsterdam and Utrecht in the north, and The Hague and Rotterdam in the south.

There are several attractive towns in Noord-Holland, as well as the city of Amsterdam. In Haarlem, the Frans Hals museum has a traditional courtyard garden and the town is a good centre from which to visit Elswout (see p.52), Beeckestijn (see p.49), and Thijsse's Hof

The large lake in the Thijsse Park at Amstelveen, near Amsterdam, planted with native plants.

in Bloemendaal (see p.65), where J P Thijsse created the first *heemtuin* or ecological garden in the 1920s. The Kennermerduinen National Park is a woodland and dune landscape, the site of several important 16th-century gardens. South of Alkmaar at Limmen there is a museum of the history of bulb growing and at Heiloo there are bulb displays in the Hortus Bulborum. Further north is the resort of Bergen, once an artists' colony and still full of galleries. Several private gardens here are open to the public including that of Sijtje Stuurman (see p.50). Aalsmeer, just south of Schiphol Airport, has the largest flower market in the world, as well as the Historische Tuin (see p.44) and Lilac Park. Before the Zuider Zee was dammed and became the fresh-water lagoon of the Ijsselmeer, Hoorn and Enkhuizen were important ports. Now they are pretty yachting towns. From Enkhuizen, where seed companies have trial grounds which can be visited, there is a road across the dyke to Lelystad in Flevoland.

Magnificent fountains at Sonsbeek Park in Arnhem.

Riet Brinkhof's charming cottage garden near Nijmegen has a collection of softly-coloured old roses.

Aalsmeer: Historische Tuin

🗄 🍽 ⊞ ♈ ♉

open: May to Sep, Tue to Thu 10am–4.30pm and Fri to Sun 1.30–4.30pm

Further information from:
Uiterweg 32, 1431 AN Aalsmeer
Tel: (0297) 322 562

Nearby sights of interest:
Also in Aalsmeer: Seringen Park in Ophelialaan is near the cemetery (Begraafplaats) and is open permanently. In this 3ha (7½ acre) park there is a good collection of lilacs, including hybrids and species from China, Himalaya, Japan, and Persia; the Daily Flower Auction takes place at the Wholesale Flower Market and visitors are welcome.

Location: Aalsmeer is SW of Amsterdam, near Schiphol Airport; well signed in Aalsmeer but you need to park in the town square, the Raadhuis plein, as there is no parking in the road near the garden

The whole history of horticulture in the Aalsmeer area is displayed in this surprisingly long and narrow garden not far from the town centre. Interesting shrubs, trees, and herbaceous plants are grown in rows on either side of a straight path that seems to stretch to infinity.

Not only have plants been rescued from extinction by an enthusiastic group of volunteers, but also garden buildings, frames, plant pots, baskets, barrows, tools, and even some of the boats that were used to transport Aalsmeer's flowers along the canals. How did the Dutch overwinter tender plants in their raw winter climate? Rich people had orangeries, but those less well-off would construct straw lean-tos. And there is an example here.

Glasshouses shelter a collection of clematis and delicate old roses such as *Rosa* 'Kaiserin Auguste Victoria' and *R.* 'Maréchal Niel'. Growing outside is the famous *R.* 'La France', the first hybrid tea, raised by Guillot of France in 1867 and *R.* 'Magna Charta' raised by Paul in Britain in 1876. There are good collections of dahlias, lilacs including *Syringa pinnatifolia*, *S. lemoine* 'Flore Pleno', and *S.* 'Rhum von Horstenstern', species roses, topiary, and peonies. These are followed by rows of trained limes, fruit trees, conifers, hollies, and other trees stretching out until the garden ends at a canal.

Examples of traditional Dutch topiary.

Kasteel Amerongen

Location: 25km (15½ miles) SE of Utrecht; take N225 Utrecht–Arnhem; at Amerongen, turn right at the traffic lights and follow the signs for the VVV

Kasteel Amerongen is tantalizingly concealed by a series of entrance gates and bridges. The first gate leads into an irregular village "square" where cars park under the trees. Inside another set of piers is the gatehouse. The garden plan suggests you return to the drive and continue to the castle but, for the gardener, there are alternative attractions: a long border of perennial plants beyond the orangery and an enticing expanse of prettily planted rose garden that slopes away in front of it.

A terraced, south-facing garden is divided into two by a low wall with a yellow border on the north side. The top section is planted with pale pink roses, and the lower section has more elaborate rose beds and rose-covered arches.

The drive to the castle continues through another set of gates and across bridges into a narrow enclosed courtyard, embellished with urns and cherubs on pedestals. This is the bastion and there is yet another bridge to cross before the forecourt where suddenly Kasteel Amerongen is revealed on the right, surrounded by a broad moat. Pyramidal yews form part of an axis to an interesting double-decker bridge across the moat to the castle. On the other side of the forecourt, past the stables, there is an iris garden and a pond. Tucked away is a tiny pavilion and secret box garden. The "north island" is a lightly wooded moated area with *stinzenflora* beneath the trees.

open: 1 Apr to 31 Oct, Tue to Fri 10am–5pm and Sat, Sun, and Public Holidays 1–5pm

Further information from:
Drostestraat 20, 3958
BK Amerongen
Tel: (0343) 454 212

Nearby sights of interest:
Amerongen: Historische Museum, Andreas Kerk; Rhenen: Cuneratoren, St Cunerkerk.

Amerongen's pretty rose garden in midsummer.

Further information from:
Prins Bernhardlaan 8, Amstelveen
Tel: (0205) 404 265

Nearby sights of interest:
Amsterdam Bospark.

Amstelveen: J P Thijsse Park

Location: From A9 Utrecht–Amsterdam road, take exit 5, Amstelveen; take the direction of Amsterdam, and the Amsterdam Bos along Kaiser Karelweg; go round a roundabout, over three canals and then turn left into a suburban housing area, continue to the roundabout and keep right; the park has several entrances

This is one of the most beautiful and successful *heemparks*. The long narrow site lies between the Amsterdam Bos and an area of suburban houses. As you enter, there is a bewildering number of paths to choose from. It is very difficult deciding between the Klamperfoliopad, Bedstropad, and Klokjespad, or the Violtjespad. Klamperfolio is honeysuckle, bedstro is bedstraw, klokjes are campanulas, and violtjes are violets. But the choice is still hard, as each seems equally attractive. These paths are often close and parallel to each other, but are astonishingly different.

You can find yourself between drifts and swathes of *Sedum acre*, harebells, ferns, mulleins, heartsease, and rosebay willow herb. Then there is an open area with seats overlooking a pond, edged with reeds and lively with moorhens. A shaded area follows and then another wonderful open path where the delicate colours of heathers can be appreciated. The streams, ponds, and paths are all sympathetically edged with logs and there is a tree cover provided by alder, oak, birch, and cornus.

Rockroses, tiny pinks, froths of Ladies' bedstraw, and *Asperula odorata* relish the light canopy of rowan and wild roses.

The flowers in this wildflower garden are planted not only in a spontaneous medley, as they occur in nature or in many other *heemtuinen*, but with art in mind. Tiny grey-leaved willows are partnered by soft mauve campanulas, harebells, and pink bell heathers. Aquilegias grow alongside two contrasting ferns, *Osmunda regalis* and *Adiantum pedatum*. At the edge of the paths are the most minute wildflowers, such as heartsease bordering sheets of *Pulmonaria officinalis* and more dramatic groups of ferns.

Wildflower gardening is not easy or a short-term option. This park has been developed since the late 1930s and a thorough knowledge of ecological conditions and processes is combined with horticultural skill and aesthetic vision. What can occur when all these abilities are combined is a revelation – and must be seen.

Royal ferns and petasites fringe one of the pools in this suburban oasis.

4 *Amsterdam: Hortus Botanicus*

Location: W of city centre on Nieuw Herengracht (canal); parking at Waterlooplein or Artis

A Hortus Medicus or physic garden – where plants were grown for medical research and to supply material for pharmacists and doctors – was in existence at the University of Amsterdam in 1638. Later botany became more important and the name was changed to Hortus Botanicus Plantage. It was laid out as a herb garden and a pleasure garden in 1682. Medicinal herbs, such as quinine and opium poppy, can still be seen in the garden, but now they are only a very small part of a remarkable collection.

The garden has water on two sides and the area is not vast, but it is crammed with 6,000 plants arranged systematically in small beds where 40 or more different plant families are represented from Aceraceae, via Liliaceae and Rosaceae to Solanaceae. There are also beds dedicated to ferns and plants of the Cape, as well as an exotic garden and small alpine scree. Water and marsh plants grow around the peat pond.

The modern three-climate glasshouse was opened in 1993, augmenting the older Indian house, cycad house, desert house, and orchid nursery. The bananas already reach the roof and appear to have been there forever. The latest addition is the high-level walkway through the temperate house from where you can look down on the tropical canopy and into a dark pool edged with brilliant orchids, ferns, and hibiscus. There is a small lift for wheel-chairs. Below there are narrow paths through dripping leaves and in the pool you can see the sacred Lotus *Nelumbo nucifera*, papyrus, and the giant waterlily *Victoria amazonica*. The sub-tropical house has southern hemisphere plants, arching tree ferns, orchids, and a *Kennedia macrophylla*, which climbs round a column reaching the roof many metres above.

open: 1 Apr to 1 Oct, Mon to Fri 9am–5pm and Sat, Sun, and Public Holidays 11am–5pm; 2 Oct to 2 Apr, Mon to Fri 9am–4pm and Sat, Sun, and Public Holidays 11am–4pm

Further information from:
Plantage Middenlaan 2a,
1018 DD Amsterdam
Tel: (0206) 258 411
Fax: (0206) 257 006

Nearby sights of interest:
Artis Zoo; Muiderpoort;
Portuguese Synagogue.

New landscaping in this 17th-century botanic garden.

open: All year, daily, sunrise to sunset

Further information from:
Stadhouderskade, Amsterdam

Nearby sights of interest:
Rijksmuseum; Stedelijk Museum; Van Gogh Museum; private gardens on the canal open occasionally on a weekend in June and Stichting de Amsterdamse Grachtentuin (tel: (0206) 392 412) will have the details.

5 *Amsterdam: Vondel Park and others*

Location: Beyond the Singel canal, near the Rijksmuseum

The oldest public park in Amsterdam was laid out in landscape style by J D and L P Zocher in 1864. Today much of the Zocher planting has disappeared but there are still oaks and willows from then, as well as swamp cypresses, a *Pterocarya stenoptera*, liquidambar, catalpa, and ginkgo to be seen among the serpentine streams and lakes. There are pavilions, flowerbeds, and a modern rose garden, and the approach is a venue for buskers, fire-eaters, and South American wind ensembles. It is jolly and lively, as a city park should be. Prins Bernhard Fons, the garden at Nederlandse Tuinenstichting, Herengracht 476, is open during office hours. Museum Willet-Holthuysen, at Herengracht 605, has an immaculate 18th-century old-Dutch-style garden, with clipped box and statues of Flora and Pomona.

---

open: Jun and Jul, Thu, Fri, and Sun, 10am–4pm; open on other days in Jun and Jul to groups, telephone to make an appointment

Further information from:
Duimeling 6, 6687 LP Angeren
Tel: (0263) 254 039

Box-edged flower borders.

6 *Angeren: De Hagenhof*

Location: S of Arnhem and NE of Nijmegen; take A15/E31 to Bemmel and then road to Huissen, after industrial zone turn right to Angeren, past two sets of crossroads to Duimeling and De Hagenhof is at the bottom on the left; from Arnhem, follow the signs to Huissen and then to Doornenburg, in village take first left over the crossroad into Duimeling

The Van Ingens have been at De Hagenhof farmhouse for 17 years but only recently have they thrown all their energies into developing the garden. The first section they made was the box garden, traditional to a farmhouse of the 19th century. Neat geometric beds are filled with white and blue flowers, and grey foliage.

Beyond the box garden are two "rooms". The Eating Garden, all yellows and bold foliage, has a sturdy table and benches built around a tree, shaded by a magnificent specimen of *Rosa* 'Easlea's Golden Rambler'. Adjacent is the Rose Garden and, on the other side of the old hawthorn hedge that borders it, a spring bulb walk.

The Apricot Garden is designed to flower after the bulbs and blossom are over. Softly coloured roses such as *R.* 'Mrs Oakley Fisher', a selection of apricot and pale

orange daylilies, a few touches of bronze foliage, and a flash of brilliant flame red, plus the lime-green of *Alchemilla mollis* are wonderfully effective.

Plans are in hand to build a new pergola by the old orchard, make a bog garden, and a new shade garden. In the meantime, the sheep and goats inhabit the parts of the garden that are not yet cultivated, a reminder of the house's past.

 # Beeckestijn

Location: 10km (6¼ miles) NE of Haarlem; take A208, then A9 in the direction of Alkmar, turn off A9 for Ijmuiden/Velsen Zuid; in Velsen Zuid turn left at traffic lights towards Velsen Broek and Beeckestijn is signed on the right after a short distance

open: At all times; museum and restaurant: All year, Wed to Sun, 12 noon to 5pm

Further information from:
Rijksweg 136, 1981 LD
Velsen-Zuid
Tel: (0255) 512 091
Fax: (0255) 511 266

Nearby sights of interest:
Haarlem: Grote Kerk of St Bavo, Stadhuis, Teyler's Museum, Frans Hals Museum; Elswout (see p.52).

A spacious and elegant formal garden on a grand scale with broad avenues and vistas.

A 14th-century farmhouse was transformed into a refined country house in the early 18th century by a rich Amsterdam merchant. A few years later he added a Régence-style garden, a mixture of French formal and English picturesque designs in which nature began to predominate. The main axis is bordered with statues and has four rows of limes each side. This imposing avenue continues to a large scalloped-shaped *bassin* enclosed by the surrounding woodland. A cross axis has a mount at one end and a pool at the other. Serpentine paths wind between geometric ranks of trees.

The French-style garden, with formal parterres and a pierced tunnel arbour, is laid out on both sides of the house. Pretty *plates-bandes* filled with flowers curve around the circular drive. On one side of the drive there are flowerbeds which are neatly kept in a slightly public parks way, blocks of lime trees, and clipped yews.

On the other side of the well-maintained house is a garden enclosed with a serpentine wall, planted with cane fruit and pear trees. Inside is a herb parterre enclosed by yew hedges. It is embellished with large tubs containing agaves and divided into sections of herbs for different purposes: magic, medicine, cooking, and dyeing.

Pretty *plates-bandes* lead the eye towards the 18th-century house.

Bergen: Sijtje Stuurman

open: Jun to Sep, Wed to Sat, 1–5.30pm; special openings: last weekend in Jun, last Sun in Jul and Aug

Further information from:
Herenweg 93, 1861 PD Bergen
Tel: (0725) 061 871

Nearby sights of interest:
Sterkenhuis Museum, Bergen;
Hortus Bulborum, Heiloo.

Location: Bergen is NE of Alkmaar, almost on the North Sea; from Bergen take the N511 towards Egmond and the garden is on the left just before Egmond

Sijtje Stuurman and her husband moved to Herenweg in 1961, taking over a house and garden both in need of much restoration. The water table in the garden is high and the ponds were full of rubbish. Only a few of the older trees remain from that time.

Today, the garden is a beautifully planted series of enclosures within enclosures. A monumental dark green hedge creates one division while other spaces are defined by tall pink plumes of astilbe, banks of rhododendrons, or a veil of weeping cherry. The high water table means that only plants which do not mind wet feet flourish from year to year. Astilbes and the pink *Sidalcea* 'Elsie Heugh' do well and ferns, hostas, and giant-leaved gunnera luxuriate in the dampness.

There is a central axial path bordered by low hedges of clipped yew which restrain pink roses from flopping onto the gravel. The focal point is a mirrored ball on a metal stand. It invites you along the path but soon there are competing scenes to entice you to one side or another: statues, arbours, or a pergola.

The flower tones are very soft, creamy or pink and mauve. There are some memorable pictures: pink *Ribes odoratus* and mauve *Malva mauritiana* are enhanced by pots of purple petunias. Tibouchina, heliotrope, pale blue lobelia, and *Vitis* 'Purpurea' all cluster round a seat painted a deep lilac. The property is surrounded by good-sized trees, including sycamores and chestnuts.

Half-hardy summer flowers in pots and baskets beautifully grouped in a corner of Sijtje Stuurman's garden.

Huis Bingerden

Location: 10km (6¼ miles) E of Arnhem, near Doesberg; from A12 Arnhem–Oberhausen motorway take exit 29 Zevenaar/Didam then direction Doesburg; at a T-junction the house is on the right

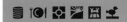

The most photographed features of the garden at Bingerden are the splendidly monumental 17th-century topiaries and yew hedges at the back. Ranks of clipped yew cubes topped with spheres and domes are set against crisply architectural hedges.

The English-style landscape park that surrounds it was designed by J P Posth in 1791. The flat fields were transformed with lakes, streams, undulations, and tree clumps in the latest fashion. Today, the groups of copper beech and an enormous plane tree are outstanding. At the far end of the garden is a mount from which there are views over dykes and meadows.

Recently Mrs van Weede, whose family has owned the estate since 1660, has been restoring the gardens and planting some attractive herbaceous borders. Against the house walls deep purple irises, pink ruffled poppies, and clematis are a soft contrast to the stark drama of the topiary. A *moestuin* is designed around a central pergola. Here, brightly coloured annuals and vegetables are laid out near to the old orchard. The designs change from year to year and you might see such pleasing partners as blue-purple cabbages with nicotiana. The pergola is clothed with roses and clematis, and underplanted with alchemilla, poppies, and *Dicentra spectabilis* 'Alba'.

open: Varies each year; write or telephone for details

Further information from:
Bingerdenseweg 21,
6986 CE Angerlo
Tel: (0313) 472 202
(Mon to Fri, 9am to 12 noon)
Fax: (0313) 475 573

Nearby sights of interest:
Kwekerij Piet Oudolf (see p.62).

17th-century yew topiary.

 # *Breukelen: Queekhoven*

Location: NW of Utrecht; take exit 5 from A2/E35, follow road into Breukelen, turning left into town at T-junction, then right; cross over the canal via the old bridge and then sharp left into Zandpad

The elegant house, orangery, and coach house are said to have been designed by Daniel Marot. The garden is equally stylish with a flowing harmony of smooth lawns, fine trees, and a sinuous stretch of water. The main effect is of an English landscape garden, but there are elements from different periods. The yew walk, with its ranks of dark, conical yews dates from the 18th century.

Everything is in scale here, and the planting is bold and simple. By the canal there is a swamp cypress and a group of hydrangeas. In another place, there is a large clump of *Gunnera manicata*. Fine trees include oaks, chestnuts, robinias, an old *Ginkgo biloba*, a *Davidia involucrata*, and some immense weeping willows. Rhododendrons add a splash of colour in May.

open: Mon to Fri, 9am–4pm

Further information from:
Zandpad 39, Breukelen

Nearby sights of interest:
Gunterstein; Nijenrode.

11

Elswout

open: At all times; the orangery: Sun, 10.30am–5.30pm

Further information from:
Elswoutlaan 23,
Bloemendaal (Overveen)
Fax: (0235) 264 152

Nearby sights of interest:
Resort of Zandvoort; city of Haarlem.

A Chinese bridge crosses the stream.

Location: W of Haarlem; from the centre of Haarlem take the direction Zandvoort and Overveen, from Overveen follow signs to Aerdenhout; Elswout is on the right but there is a one-way system in operation here and it is necessary to continue round Duinlustweg, continue left and double back

Elswout is one of the many properties where elaborate formal gardens were swept away in favour of an English-style landscape park. Described thus "No other country house built on a virgin site displays such a striking and harmonious design of house and garden, inspired by classical and Italian examples" (Erik de Jong), there are now only tantalizing reminders of what it must have been like. Gabriel van Marcelis acquired the estate in 1654 and by 1657 had built the house and garden. Nobody knows exactly who created this much-admired ensemble but it has been attributed to Jacob van Campen.

In the late 18th century, Johan Georg Michael designed a new park of open meadowland, with clumps of trees, natural ponds, and winding streams. The vast, almost derelict mansion looks down upon pavilions, monumental steps, balustrades, and Chinese and Swiss bridges crossing the water. There are fine avenues of beech and lime throughout the park, and on each side of a central grassed field at the front. The wooded grounds contain many footpaths and autumn colour is particularly fine.

12

Kasteel De Haar

open: All year except 16 Aug to second Sun in Oct, daily, 9am–5pm
open: 3 Jan to 14 Mar, Sun, 1–4pm; 16 Mar to 30 May, Tue to Sun, 1–4pm; 31 May to 22 Aug, Mon to Fri 11am–4pm and Sat and Sun 1–4pm; 3 Oct to 14 Nov, Tue to Sun, 1–4pm; 15 Nov to 31 Nov, Sun, 1–4pm

Further information from:
Kasteellaan 1, 3455 RR Haarzuilens
Tel: (0306) 771 275

Nearby sights of interest:
Utrecht: Domtoren, Kloostegang and Kloostertuin, Rijksmuseum including Het Catherijne Convent.

Location: NW of Utrecht; from A2/E35 take exit Maarssen/Vleuten, direction Vleuten and then Haarzuilens and the castle is signed; from A12/E30 take exit 15, De Meern, then follow road to Vleuten

It might be better not to read this but to emerge from the surrounding wood without any expectations at all. Then the fairy-tale castle would seem even more unexpectedly breathtaking. The tall building is amazingly beautiful and looks so genuine it is a surprise to learn that it is a late 19th-century restoration.

What we see today was the inspiration of Baron Etienne de Haar who inherited a ruin with little land from his father. He married the Baroness Hélène de Rothschild, adding wealth to a passion for the late medieval period, when the Van Zuylens, from whom he was descended, were at their peak. He began to re-purchase and re-create the entire estate. The architect he chose was the Gothic Revival architect, P J H Cuypers.

The gardens were designed at the same time, ostensibly by Henri Copijn but with most of the formal garden actually by Cuypers. Copijn was responsible for the landscape-style park with lakes, vistas, and tree clumps. He had 7,000 40-year-old trees transplanted to De Haar to create an instant park at the end of the 19th century.

The fairy-tale castle De Haar.

The formal gardens comprise a box *parterre de broderie*, a formal rose garden, the Roman garden, and a magnificent grand canal. The Roman garden illustrates the success of the collaboration of Cuypers and Copijn, where domed yews lead the eye to out beyond the garden into the park.

Behind the castle, on a separate island, is a pie-plate of pink and white begonias and a bastion which enables one to look across the canal and into the deer park.

 ## *Hernen: De Brinkhof*

Location: 16km (10 miles) W of Nijmegen; from A50 's-Hertogenbosch–Nijmegen take exit Wijchen, then at T-junction turn right direction Bergharen; from Nijmegen take the exit to Nilftrik/Grave/Wijchen and follow signs to Bergharen, after 2.5km (1½ miles), centre of Hernen, turn right and immediately right again before church and the house is on the right

open: 1 Apr to 15 Oct, Thu, Fri, and Sat 10am–5pm

Further information from:
Dorpsstraat 46, 6616AJ Hernen
Tel: (0487) 531 486

Nearby sights of interest:
Kasteel Hernen at Dorpsstraat 40, Hernen, tel: (0487) 531 387, is open from 15 Apr to 1 Nov, Tue, Thu, and Sat 10am to 12 noon and 2–5pm; the garden is also open on special garden days.

The garden at De Brinkhof has a noteworthy collection of roses and many interesting planting ideas. Its particular magic, however, comes from historic and symbolic features that you scarcely notice but which give the garden an underlying resonance. Like a good book, it lives in the mind long after the covers have been closed.

Like many gardeners who love unusual plants, Riet Brinkhof was faced with the challenge of placing them so the overall effect was not bitty. She has solved this by colour-theming the borders. The 17th-century farmhouse is painted a traditional dark slaty colour and one border that goes from blue to mauve to pink shows up beautifully against the sombre walls.

A small wooded area has made a perfect spring garden. Bulbs and hellebores do well before the leaves open and crowd out the sun. A pear tree is underplanted with snowdrops for the winter and in the summer has a skirt of frothy lime-green alchemilla.

Flowering in the shade of the large American oak are roses and geraniums. The velvety dark red *Rosa* 'Charles de Mills' is placed next to a copper hazel and the pink roses *R.* 'Albertine', *R.* 'Chaucer', and *R.* 'Dainty Bess' are planted among the elegant spikes of *Veronicastrum* 'Lucette'.

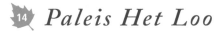

🍁 14 *Paleis Het Loo*

Location: N of Apeldoorn, just beyond the ring road; well signed

open: All year, daily,
10am–5pm; closes Mon
except Bank Holidays
open: As above

Further information from:
Koninklijk Park 1,
7315 JA Apeldoorn
Tel: (0555) 772 400
Fax: (0555) 219 983

Nearby sights of interest:
Kroller-Muller Museum and
Sculpture Park – good collection
of Van Gogh.

Just as the recent restoration of the Privy Garden at Hampton Court outside London occasioned some controversy, so too did the work done to the Baroque garden at Het Loo between 1977 and 1984. Both are William and Mary gardens, dating from the mid-17th century, which had changed radically over the years. The public had grown accustomed to seeing large trees in a park-like setting. What was proposed was a return to the most exquisitely formal of gardens.

In 1684, William Prince of Orange bought the medieval castle of Het Oude Loo. A year later the building of a new palace began. No one knows who designed the buildings or the garden layout but the king's architect, Jacob Roman, supervised the construction and Daniel Marot was also closely involved. His characteristic Baroque flourishes can be seen in the designs of the parterres.

Plates-bandes surround a box parterre.

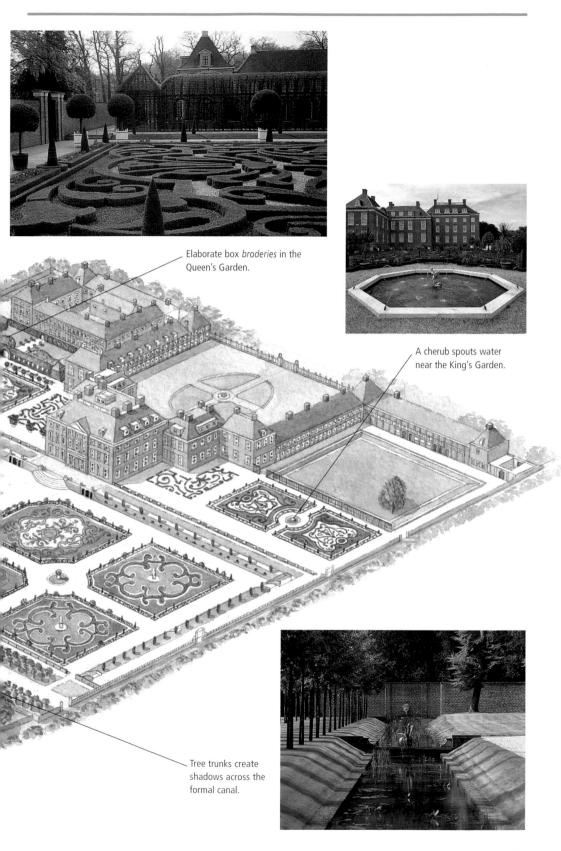

Elaborate box *broderies* in the Queen's Garden.

A cherub spouts water near the King's Garden.

Tree trunks create shadows across the formal canal.

Beyond the Fountain of Venus are the King's Fountain and the curved colonnade, which terminates the main axis.

William had married the English Princess Mary, daughter of James II, in 1677 and had an English physician, Walter Harris. It is thanks to Harris that we have a detailed description of the gardens at Het Loo exactly as they were constructed. In 1688 William and Mary were invited to become King and Queen of England and although Mary did not return to Holland after that, William frequently did. Work at Het Loo continued until 1695.

The lower or sunken garden was surrounded on three sides by high terraces, from where the design of the elaborate box parterres and *plates-bandes* could be clearly seen. There were eight parterres around a Fountain of Venus. A cross axis had on one side of the fountain a Celestial Globe Fountain and a Terrestrial Globe on the other. There were water cascades from the high terraces to the lower level. The upper garden and the main axis terminated with a curved colonnade and were spectacularly decorated with two fountains, the King's Fountain and the Peacock Fountain, and busts of Roman Emperors. Fourteen box-edged beds of flowers surrounded the King's Fountain.

Next to the Palace, outside their respective quarters, were the King's Garden with a bowling green and the Queen's Garden.

This grand garden was partly changed into an English-style landscape park by subsequent Princes of Orange. Then during the Napoleonic wars, Willem V, the Prince of Orange, fled to England and Napoleon's brother, Louis Napoleon, completed the destruction of the formal garden, by knocking down walls and staircases and selling statues. Beech and oak trees were planted and the transformation to a *parc à l'anglaise* completed.

When the garden was restored, just four parterres were replaced around the King's Fountain in the upper garden because it was decided to compromise total authenticity and retain some of the particularly fine trees, including a *Liriodendron tulipfera* and some copper beeches, from the landscape park era.

The Queen's Garden too is not exactly as it was. Buildings had been erected over part of it and the restoration work on the Palace did not include removing these. The garden is still delightful, however, with gravel walks shaded by huge hornbeam tunnel-arbours, beds of flowers, and espaliered fruit trees trained along the walls. The King's Garden is a bowling green again, with more parterres of flowers, clipped box, and juniper.

A particularly interesting part of the restoration has been the planting of the *plates-bandes*, or double box hedges, punctuated with elegantly trimmed junipers, with authentic plants of the 17th century. Again, Harris had listed the plants that were grown and much work was done tracking down the identical species or finding appropriate substitutes. Flowers include *Rosa mundi*, crown imperials, monkshood, dictamnus, rue, flag irises, peonies, and *Acanthus mollis*. These are all planted in the narrow beds between the box at some distance from each other. Each plant was treated like a rare jewel and given an individual setting.

More than a dozen years after the restoration was completed, the garden still looked as if had only just been finished. If one had a wish, it would be that nature would be given a little leeway and allowed to soften some of the outlines as it surely must have done originally.

The Terrestrial Globe Fountain.

Water flows over an ornate cascade from a raised terrace to pools and fountains on the lower level.

open: All year, Mon to Thu 10am–6pm, Fri 10am–9pm, and Sat 10am–5pm

Further information from:
"de Hof van Heden",
Purmerenderweg 44, 1461 DD
Zuidoost Beemster
Tel: (0299) 681 537
Fax: (0299) 681 602

Nearby sights of interest:
Beemster Arboretum.

A formal display garden.

 # *Koelemeijer Tuinen*

Location: N of Purmerend which is 15km (9¼ miles) N of Amsterdam; from A7/E22 Zaandam (Amsterdam ring) to Hoorn and Leeuwarden, take exit 5, Purmerend/Zuidoost/Beemster, direction Purmerend, then second left direction Oosthuizen (this is Purmerend way) and the gardens are 3km (2 miles) on the left, through the garden centre

To find the display gardens here you have to first make your way round an enormous garden centre. The model gardens are in a diversity of styles, in different shapes, and with varied planting. The 30 areas range from a Dutch herb garden, a town garden, a box garden, a water garden, a modern garden with decking, and rock gardens to a Japanese garden which incorporates nothofagus, bamboo, and distinctive parasol pines.

There are unusual planting ideas – catalpas and Judas trees grow from the centre of cubes of clipped yew – and the wide variety of plants of all types are well grown. There are arbours, pools, shade gardens, colour borders, woodland gardens, and sitting places – in fact every type of garden you can think of, including some with very grand features, modest family gardens, formal areas, an ultra fashionable grass and bamboo garden, and many displaying sculpture, garden furniture, and other ornaments, and all on a small scale. No one with a small garden could fail to find something of interest here.

open: Apr to Oct, first weekend in the month, 10am–5pm; guided tours available for groups of 20 or over (telephone to make a booking), Apr to mid-Oct, daily

Further information from:
Oud Over 154a, 3632 VH
Loenen a/d Vecht
Tel: (0294) 231 572

Nearby sights of interest:
River Vecht; Over-Holland.

 # *Loenen: Terra Nova*

Location: W of Hilversum and NE of Utrecht, on eastern bank of the River Vecht N of Loenen; from A2/E35 Utrecht–Amsterdam motorway take exit 4, Vinkenveen, direction Loenen and in Loenen where road turns right, cross canal and turn left; Terra Nova is on the left after some distance

Terra Nova is a magical wood and water garden, with streams and small bridges and long fingers of land that stretch out into the Loosdrechtse.

Throughout the woodland walk exotic trees, such as sophoras, catalpa, *Ginkgo biloba*, pink magnolias, the tulip tree (*Liriodendron tulipfera*), and a swamp cypress, mingle unselfconsciously with native trees. In a clearing there is a formal rose garden with arches, conical yews, and a central statue of Hebe, cup bearer of the gods. Three *Pterocarya fraxinifolia*, the Caucasian wing-nut, stand along one side of the geometric layout.

The path continues past a large sculptured group that came from St Petersburg, beside a circular carp pond, along a stream bank planted with hydrangeas, by a row of white horse chestnuts to the lake edge. Waterlilies, including the yellow false waterlily (*Nuphar lutea*), and islands seem to float into the silvery distance. Long fillets of land and water interlock round the shore.

At the furthest point of the walk is a turreted octagonal wooden tea-house surrounded by rhododendrons and wildflowers. The return route is along a deck walk around the edge of the water. *Petasites japonica*, willow, alders, reeds, and meadowsweet colonize the damp ground and provide shelter for moorhens, ducks, and dragonflies.

 # *Maarssen: May Hobijn*

Location: Maarssen is NW of Utrecht and the garden is between Maarssen and Breukelen; from Breukelen turn right before the Begraafplaats (cemetery); from Maarssen turn left directly after the Begraafplaats

May Hobijn opens her garden for two months every summer while it is host to a sculpture exhibition. Pieces of modern art by a variety of artists are displayed round the garden.

The garden is boldly planted with flower borders that are an excitable mixture of herbaceous plants, bulbs, tubers, and roses. Sometimes this can result in quite riveting colour combinations, like one group of diascia, African marigolds, yellow and red bronze-leaved dahlias, and peachy coloured daylilies. Another unforgettable planting consisted of *Rosa mutabilis*, the purple-leaved orach, *Atriplex atropurpurea*, red achillea, orange lilies, deep crimson monarda, and dark red daylilies.

The house, which dates from 1700, consists of linked coach house and stable buildings with an inner courtyard where there is a formal box garden and central pool. A roof terrace enables you to see the main flower garden from above and also to look over the wall to the Vecht on the far side of the road.

There are gardens on all sides, with a semi-wild garden, where poppies seed themselves among *Salvia horminum*, Japanese anemones and hydrangeas, shade borders, and a fern garden. In one area outside the garden wall, in the narrow strip between it and a tiny road-side dyke, there are trained fruit trees and flowerbeds neatly edged with box. Other features include a square rock garden with various sempervivums, about 100 roses, and a fine mulberry.

The artworks frequently clash with the extrovert borders. It would be good to see the garden without them.

open: Last week in May, Jun, Jul, mid-Aug, Fri, Sat, and Sun, 12 noon to 5pm; for groups of ten or more telephone to make an appointment

Further information from:
Straatweg 31, 3603 CV Maarssen
Tel: (0346) 560 518

Nearby sights of interest:
Goudesteyn (Maarssen Town Hall).

Rich colours and bold shapes are typical of May Hobijn's planting.

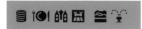

open: Variable, telephone
(085) 610 616 to enquire

Further information from:
Landgoed Middachten 3,
6994 JC De Steeg
Tel: (0264) 954 998
Fax: (0264) 955 115

Nearby sights of interest:
Kasteel Rosendael (see pp.62–3);
Huis Bingerden (see p.51);
Nederlands Openlucht Museum
Kruidentuin (see p.61).

The 17th-century castle seen
from the south parterre.

18 *Kasteel Middachten*

Location: SW of Dieren, between Zutphen and Arnhem on N348; from A48 take exit 3, De Steeg, and follow directions to Dieren; Middachten is on the provincial road between De Steeg and Dieren and when you reach the avenues of trees that indicate a historic estate, look carefully for the entrance to Middachten on the right

Kasteel Middachten was designed by Jacob Roman and Steven Vennecool in 1694 on the foundations of an older building. It sits proudly in the middle of a broad moat approached by a bridge from a grand *cour d'honneur* flanked by stables and outbuildings.

The garden is a cruciform design with an open area opposite each façade of the castle and more intricate features and enclosed gardens in the corners. There is constant progression from space to enclosure as you walk around the garden. As you enter through the gate in the west-facing wall there is a sunken lawn with two herbaceous borders. To the left of the sunken lawn is a tennis lawn surrounded by a trellis, a croquet lawn, and a parterre of bedded-out flowers. A thatched summerhouse is a sudden reminder that although the garden was originally laid out in the 18th century, many of the best-known landscape designers of the late 19th and 20th century are reckoned to have had a hand in its redesign.

On the right of the sunken lawn are a green theatre and a striking yew maze. The south parterre lies between the moat and the canal. In the next corner is the formal rose garden and this is followed by an English-style lawn with trees and rhododendrons. The final corner has a regular lawn with specimen ginkgos, a herb garden, and adjacent to it, in front of the orangery, a flower garden decorated with orange trees in blue and white tubs.

---

open: 15 Apr to 1 Nov, daily
except Mon, 10am–6pm

Further information from:
Klaverland 9, 6566 JD Millingen
aan de Rijn
Tel and fax: (0481) 431 885

Nearby sights of interest:
River Rhine; Bergen Dal;
African Museum; De Hagenhof
(see pp.48–9).

19 *Millinger Theetuin*

Location: 5km (3 miles) E of Nijmegen between villages of Kekerdom and Millingen aan de Rijn; the tea-garden can only be reached on foot through the nature reserve Millingerwaard; public transport: bus 80 or 81 from Nijmegen Central Station, alight Kekerdom church, after 50m (164ft) on the right, follow the signs and it is a 2km (1¼ mile) walk

The garden is situated in an ancient Dutch river-landscape. It was part of an old brickworks and the owners, Coen and Floor, have been developing it for about ten years. They have tried to achieve a garden like those found in warmer climates where much of life takes place outside, a challenge in Nijmegen where winters can be severe.

A curving concrete staircase, decorated with tiles and leading to a covered verandah looks positively Portuguese. A path paved with flat river stones is like an alley in a Greek village. A wall of old Dutch brick has been washed with the palest sand-coloured limewash and looks permanently sunny.

The planting in the borders is luxuriant: hydrangea, white-flowering valerian, polemonium, and delphiniums compete with each other. There is a mixture of hardy perennials and bold tender plants which gives the southern Mediterranean effect. Pots containing lemon trees, *Tibouchina urvilleana*, canna lilies, and even palms, stand out in a courtyard against ivy-covered walls and yucca contrasts with delphiniums in this very successful garden.

---

20 *Nederlands Openlucht Museum Kruidentuin*

Location: N of Arnhem; well signed from E35/A12 motorway from Den Haag and Utrecht and from A50/N50 from Zwolle and Apeldoorn; from centre of Arnhem, follow signs to Apeldoorn and museum is signed

open: Apr to Oct, daily, 10am–5pm; guided tours of herb garden Jun and Jul, Tue, 5–7pm

Further information from:
Schelmseweg 89, 6816 SJ Arnhem
Tel: (0263) 576 100

Nearby sights of interest:
Burger's Dierenpark (zoo); Kasteel Rosendael (see pp.62–3); Arnhem.

This open-air museum contains traditional buildings, houses, windmills, and bridges from all over the Netherlands.

The museum herb garden has a comprehensive range of plants grown in attractive surroundings. Enclosed by old brick walls and divided internally with hornbeam hedges it is laid out mainly in the Renaissance style. The garden is centred around a Baroque iron pump that stands in the middle of a luxuriant mass of angelica, iris, and verbascum. In the medieval monastery garden brick-edged beds contain sage, rue, lovage, marrubium, and mentha. The largest section of the garden consists of small rectangular beds containing medicinal herbs organized according to their purpose: for example, sedatives and liver complaints. In the culinary herb garden, which is designed like an old-style Dutch farm garden, herbs are grown for seasoning and there are traditional vegetables and other plants which had a particular function in the home.

The Box Clock is a fascinating feature in the herb garden.

There is an intriguing Box Clock with tiles for each month. You stand on the tile for the month and your shadow is meant to strike the correct hour "written" in *Buxus sempervirens*.

In the nursery the plants used in the herb garden and around the houses are propagated. The plants are not for sale. There are many old-fashioned perennial plants, as well as a fruit garden where rootstocks for use in grafting are cultivated.

21 *Kwekerij Piet Oudolf*

Location: E of Arnhem, between Zutphen and Doetinchem via N314; in Hummelo take road to Toldijk; Broekstraat is on left about halfway between the two villages

open: All year, Tue to Sat, 10am–4pm and by appointment; nursery: all year, Tue to Sat, 10am–4pm

Further information from:
Broekstraat 17, 6999 DE Hummelo
Tel: (0314) 381 120

Nearby sights of interest:
Grote Kerk, Doetinchem.

A subtle mix of flowers and grasses.

Piet Oudolf is well known in Europe as the grower of desirable hardy herbaceous plants. He is also a garden designer and the nursery is divided into two, with a private garden at the front and the nursery at the back.

It is the plant combinations that Oudolf does so exceptionally well that make the garden memorable. None of the plants are difficult to grow but they are subtly different cultivars associated in a new way. There are various astrantias in colours ranging from deep crushed strawberry to dark red planted near bronze-leaved *Euphorbia dulcis* 'Chaemeleon'. *Aesculus parviflora* seems to compete with large clumps of *Polygonum polymorphum*. Many of the perennials are large: eupatoriums, tall *Miscanthus sinensis*, the polygonum just mentioned, even *Sedum* 'Matrona' can be described as stout and tall. They are planted where other gardens would use shrubs and the effects are striking.

Among the ever-changing appearance of the perennial plants, is the occasional piece of permanent plant architecture. Yew hedges are planted in diagonal lines like the wings of a stage and silver-leaved pear is clipped into rectangular columns.

22 *Kasteel Rosendael*

Location: NE edge of Arnhem; from A12/E35 take exit 26, Arnhem Noord, direction Velp Rozendaal; from Arnhem centre follow directions to Apeldoorn; outside boundary of town, Rozendaal is signed; drive into village and park on left before roundabout at the bottom; take road signed Begraafplaats and Bedriegertjies

open: 1 May to 1 Nov, Tue to Sat 10am–6pm and Sun 1–6pm

Further information from:
Rosendael 1, 6891 DA Rozendaal
Tel: (0263) 644 645

Nearby sights of interest:
Burger's Dierenpark (zoo); Nederlands Openlucht Museum Kruidentuin (see p.61); Nationaal Park de Hoge Veluwe.

Although the castle at Rosendael dates from the 14th century (the round tower survives from then), the gardens were not made until Janne and Jan van Arnhem, friends of William and Mary, inherited the house in 1667. Jan van Arnhem is believed to have designed waterworks, parterres, and some garden ornaments.

The Arnhems had no children and the estate was inherited by their nephew, Lubbert Torck, in 1721. He renovated and added to the house and employed Daniel Marot to modernize the garden layout. Marot did not alter the basic design but added the shell gallery, the shell grotto, the gazebo, the trick fountains (the *bedriegertjes*), and the large sculpted cascade.

The garden was first touched by the fashion for the landscape style in 1781 but it was not until 1834 that it was completely changed. J D Zocher the younger designed the park that we see today, fortunately retaining Marot's *fabriques*. Many of the features, including the shell gallery and the orangery, were badly damaged during World War II.

It was not until 1972 that the repair of the shell gallery was undertaken. It is a semicircular construction, made up of two quadrants with a cascade in the centre. In each quadrant are niches with either fountains or benches and a pavilion, all of which are exquisitely covered with intricate designs in about 16 different kinds of shell, mother of pearl, and blue stones that resemble lapis lazuli. Mollusc shells are lined with plumes in mother of pearl and large pink conch shells are used to create rose shapes, to symbolize Rosendael.

Daniel Marot's elaborate shell gallery magnificently restored.

In 1978 Rosendael was left to the charity Het Geldersch Landschap, and between 1984 and 1986 the park was completely restored. Vistas were opened up, lawns resown, and ponds and the spring fed streams on which the water features depend were re-bottomed with waterproof clay. In 1996 the trick fountains and the shell grotto were restored.

The garden at Rosendael has recovered the appearance it must have had at the beginning of the century with three informally shaped lakes on different levels, linked by cascades and waterfalls, and with jokes such as the chain bridge, trick fountains, and exquisite Baroque follies dispersed in a slightly incongruous setting.

---

23 *Slot Zuylen*

Location: Oud Zuilen is just NW of Utrecht; from A2/E35 to Amsterdam, take exit Maarssen/Utrecht Noord and then keep right on N230, not left into Maarssen, and follow signs to Oud Zuilen and the castle

Slot Zuylen is a picturesque moated castle with four octagonal corner towers dating from c1520. The outstanding feature of the garden is the long crinkle-crankle wall. It could be marvellous, but sadly it is rather neglected. Against the serpentine wall in only some of the "bays" are nectarines, vines, and peaches, and not all these plants are carefully pruned. Opposite are blocks of what seem to be forgotten dahlias, alchemilla, peonies, and daylilies. Between this cutting garden and the moat are some ancient espaliered pear trees with gnarled trunks.

There is an orchard and a box parterre in an oval surrounded by columnar pear trees. In the box parterre are *plates-bandes* with the plants spaced in typical William and Mary style. The park in the English landscape style was laid out c1840 by J D Zocher.

open: When castle is open
open: 15 Mar to 15 May and 15 Sep to 15 Nov, Tue, Wed, Thu 11am–5pm and Sat and Sun 2–5pm; guided tours: 15 May to 15 Sep, Tue to Thu 11am, 1pm, and 4pm, Fri 11am, Sat 2–4pm, Sun 1–4pm

Further information from:
Tournooiveld 1, 3611 AS
Oud Zuilen
Tel: (0302) 440 255

Nearby sights of interest:
Utrecht: cathedral, museums, galleries; Kasteel Groeneveld; Cantonpark, Baarn.

open: At all times

Further information from:
Apeldoornseweg, Arnhem
Tel: (026) 368 7911 (council)

Nearby sights of interest:
Arnhem: Municipal Museum,
St Walpurgisbasiliek, Belvedere;
Witte Molen (watermill); garden
of Mrs L Kloeg at 6 Braamweg,
Arnhem, tel: (026) 442 4730 for
appointment from 15 April to
end of June.

24 *Sonsbeek and Zypendaal Parks*

Location: From centre of Arnhem, follow signs to Apeldoorn and as road begins
to climb, Sonsbeek Park is on the left

Sonsbeek is a beautiful park covering 68ha (168 acres), originally
laid out in 1742 and planted with majestic beeches, oaks, and
rhododendrons. There are walks through the woods, a lake with
fountain jets, and several other large linked expanses of water.

This park adjoins the estate of Zypendaal where a sweeping
expanse of grass with a magnificent clump of five great copper
beeches adjoins the attractive moated castle. There are pleasant
woods for walking in but this area, contoured, proportioned, and
simple, is what landscape parks are about. It is not huge but the
effect is one of exhilarating spaciousness. Opposite the castle are
two symmetrical pavilions separated by an ornamental parterre.

---

open: Apr, Sat, Sun, and
Public Holidays, 12 noon to
5pm; May to Sep, Tue to Fri
10am–5pm and Sat, Sun, and
Public Holidays 12 noon to 5pm;
Oct, Sat and Sun, 12 noon to 5pm

Further information from:
Nieuw-Loosdrechtsedijk 150,
1231 LC Nieuw-Loosdrecht
Tel: (0355) 823 208

Nearby sights of interest:
Kasteel Groeneveld.

The box parterre.

25 *Kasteel–Museum Sypesteyn*

Location: W of Hilversum; from A27/E311 take exit Hilversum, then N201 ring road;
follow signs to Nieuw-Loosdrecht; Sypestein is well signed

The romantic castle was built in the early 20th century by Henry
van Sypesteyn on the foundations of what he believed to be his
ancestral home, which had been destroyed by the armies of
Louis XIV of France between 1672 and 1673. The garden was
also laid out by Jhr van Sypesteyn at the same time in the style
of the late 16th and early 17th century.

The central formal garden is on the castle island and is
reached by two stone bridges. Inside there is a pear pergola and
within that, behind attractive wrought-iron gates, is a pretty box
parterre planted with herbaceous plants such as sedums and
echinacea. This area is surrounded by hornbeam, pleached limes,
and sweet chestnuts. There are several
interesting exotic trees, including *Cercis
siliquastrum*, the tulip tree *Liriodendron
tulipfera*, *Ailanthus altissima*, *Cladrastis
lutea*, and a dramatic weeping sophora.

At the end of an orchard on the other
side of the moat from the castle, where
there are newly planted quince and
walnut trees, there is a tiny topiary
garden. In the flowerbeds nearby astilbes
and hostas are grown in blocks. Behind, a

patte d'oie of three paths points the way either into the woodland or to the *doolhof*. This hornbeam labyrinth has a *Sorbus aria* planted in the middle of it. The estate extends into the countryside and there are different areas of woodland trees, one of yew and rhododendron, an oak wood, and a wood with a beech lane that is recorded on 18th-century maps.

26 *Thijsse's Hof*

Location: Bloemendaal is NW of Haarlem; take N200 to Zandvoort; at Overveen, follow directions to Bloemendaal and continue along the main road for about 1.5km (1 mile); Mollaan is on the left

open: 1 Apr to 31 Oct, Tue to Sat 9am–5pm, Sun 9am–1pm; 1 Nov to 30 Mar, Tue to Sat, 9am–4pm; closes 24 Dec to 2 Jan

Further information from:
Mollaan 4, 2061 BD Bloemendaal
Tel: (0235) 262 700

Nearby sights of interest:
Nationaal Park de Kennermeduinen;
Haarlem: Frans Hals Museum,
Teyler's Museum, St Bavokerk.

Dutch teacher and biologist J P Thijsse (1865–1945) saw that much of the natural environment of Holland was under threat from expanding industry and housing, and felt that public parks and gardens did not replace the countryside. In 1925 Thijsse, together with his gardener and landscape architect Leonard Springer, created a natural garden which drew on the new sciences of botanical geography and plant ecology and was the forerunner of all the *heemparks* and *heemtuins* in Holland.

The garden contains different environments, including water, woodland, heath, and even a cereal field. Paths wind around a central pond and the site is surrounded by dune-type woodland. Some of the grassland is mown, and some left to flower. There is a bee demonstration cabinet and hive and a demonstration strip of blocks of wildflowers. Many plants are labelled but with Dutch common names only. A good dictionary or a Dutch wildflower guide which gives Latin names will be helpful.

The birth place of the *heemtuin* or ecological garden.

 open: 1 Mar to 30 Nov, Mon
to Fri 9am–5pm and Sat and Sun
10am–5pm

Further information from:
Budapestlaan 17, Utrecht,
De Uithof
Tel: (0302) 531 826

Nearby sights of interest:
Utrecht: cathedral, art galleries,
and museums.

**Conifers and boulders are a
contrast to the sun-loving flowers.**

Utrecht: Fort Hoofddijk Universiteit Botanische Tuinen

Location: Take A28/E30 to Amersfoort then exit 2, De Uithof, the University
campus; follow signs to De Uithof and the botanic garden is signed

The University of Utrecht has owned Fort Hoofddijk since 1964.
The fort was once part of the defences of Utrecht and dates from
1879. The bunkers form the foundations of the largest rock garden
in Europe. The garden has recently been extended and now
comprises the systematic garden, the *buitenfort* where there are
Dutch native plants, the research collection garden with tropical
and subtropical greenhouses, and the theme gardens.

The steep mound of the rock garden is terraced with logs and
moss and all the plants are labelled. Species from many parts of
the world grow in separate areas, while cultivars are planted at
the beginning of the garden. Tucked down at the bottom there
is a small alpine house, surrounded by troughs with more alpines
such as the pretty yellow-flowered *Verbascum* 'Letitia'.

The systematic garden has a modern layout of hexagonal
beds, a representation of the major plant families and their
mutual relationship. In part of the glasshouse complex there is
a collection of plants from South America, a Utrecht speciality.

Beyond the glasshouse the path leads to the newest area, the
theme gardens. These were landscaped by Arda Wijsbek and
opened in 1995. The themes range from landscape to religion
and there is even a vampire garden. This area also contains a
beautiful flowering meadow, a wisteria pergola with a pretty
border of thickly planted annuals, and a Japanese water garden.

 open: All year, Mon to Fri
9am–5pm and Sat and Sun
10am–5pm

Further information from:
Vossesteinsesteeg 8, Doorn
Tel: (0302) 531 826

Nearby sights of interest:
Huis Doorn, the home of the last
Kaiser of Germany, William II, is
surrounded by a landscape park.

Von Gimborn Arboretum

Location: SE of Utrecht; from A12/E36 Utrecht to Arnhem motorway, take exit
Driebergen, direction Doorn; the arboretum is signed

The arboretum is named after its founder, Max von Gimborn,
who was an ink manufacturer, and designed by a landscape
architect called Bleeker. It was always meant to be both
landscape park and arboretum combined around a dwelling
house, but the house was never built.

Von Gimborn hoped to establish a definitive collection of
conifers. He was also interested in ericaceous plants and laid out
a large heather garden in the centre of the arboretum. After

World War II, the arboretum began to deteriorate and only a famous tsuga wood and the heather garden were kept in order.

After von Gimborn's death in 1964, the arboretum became the property of the University of Utrecht. The university had discovered that the soil at Fort Hoofddijk (see opposite) was unsuitable for an arboretum and the von Gimborn arboretum complemented the new botanic garden at De Uithof well. Today the arboretum has been returned to its past glory. Most of the plants are labelled, some of them after much research among experts. The university is concentrating on building up its collections of Aceraceae, Betulacea, Coniferae, Ericaceae, Oleaceae and the generas Euonymus, Laburnum, and Magnolia.

In all seasons there is much to see, from the peeling bark of *Prunus serrula* and winter-flowering heathers in January, magnolias and acers in April, the lilac-purple azalea *Rhododendron* 'Amoenum' and *R. mollis* cultivars in May to horse chestnuts in August and splendid colour from amelanchiers, larches, and liquidambars from September to the frosts.

Wooded areas are interspersed with glades in the arboretum.

29 *Wageningen: Belmonte and Driejen Botanische Tuinen*

Location: Leave Utrecht Arnhem motorway E12 at exit 24, Wageningen, and onto N781; cross first and second sets of traffic lights; at the first intersection after, turn left for Belmonte or right for De Driejen (two blocks up)

open: At all times

Further information from:
Landbouwuniversiteit
Wageningen, Generaal
Foulkesweg 94, 6700 ED
Wageningen
and also PO Box 8010,
6700 ED Wageningen
Tel: (0317) 483 160

Nearby sights of interest:
Kasteel Duurstede Park; Kasteel
Doorwerth; Kasteel Renswoude.

The estate at Belmonte was bought by the government in 1951 so that the Agricultural University at Wageningen could establish an arboretum there. The Italianate country house and grounds dating from 1843 had been destroyed in 1945.

Planting began in 1953 and although the main objectives of this botanic garden are education and science, the visual aspects of the landscape have not been ignored. As the name Belmonte suggests, this is a hill and there are fine views – rare in the Netherlands – of the surrounding countryside.

With trees and shrubs from all over the world, there is always something in bloom. The season begins with winter-flowering heathers, *Erica carnea* cultivars, and witch hazels, followed by *Corylopsis* ssp., forsythia and mahonias in spring, and a crescendo in early summer with rhododendrons, magnolias, and many flowering cherries and crabs. In autumn, there are the colourful leaves of acers, rosehips, and many berries.

There are fine acers and good groups of fothergillas, witch hazels, and euonymus. A clump of different hawthorns includes *Crategeus submollis* 'Sargentia' with 7.5cm (3in) long spines. *Quercus dentata* 'Murray' is underplanted effectively with the low-growing forsythia 'Arnold Dart' (syn. 'Arnold Dwarf').

Nearby De Dreijen was the experimental garden attached to the first landscape gardening school, a precursor of today's Agricultural University of Wageningen. It was designed at the end of the 19th century by Leonard Springer and remains of his arboretum still exist just east of the pond in the rock garden.

This is a particularly good botanic garden for the amateur gardener. The systematic beds contain a large collection of perennial plants arranged alphabetically according to family. Plants such as *Mirabilis jalapa* are trialled. Medicinal and dye-producing plants grow in a kitchen garden. More than 600 species roses are at their best in June, and these are accompanied by a large collection of moss roses including *Rosa* 'Nuits de Young' and *R.* 'Blanc Mousseaux'. Many of the roses grow near a central formal feature laid out around a bust of Linnaeus.

Specimen trees and shrubs are underplanted with wildflowers and grasses at Belmonte.

De Hof van Walenburg

Location: SE of Utrecht; take N225 in direction of Arnhem and at Doorn turn south on N227 to Langbroek; the garden is well signed on open days

As you enter Walenburg, Sissinghurst Castle in south-east England instantly springs to mind. A romantic medieval tower overlooks the garden in the same way and the lavish planting, dense with old roses, reinforces the impression. There are of course differences. The tower is attached to a 16th-century house and it stands, with a small surrounding garden on an island in a moat, separated from the garden by a bridge. The garden was designed in 1965 by the architect E A Canneman and his wife, Mrs M E Canneman. The cruciform design is based on a main axis from the tower and the bridge and a cross axis which creates four "rooms" around a semi-enclosed circle in the centre.

The first room contains a greenhouse and a collection of tender plants in pots on one side, a herb garden, and mixture of delphiniums and roses on the other. Outside the greenhouse, the planting is in soft colours: pink cleomes, *Lavatera* 'Barnsley', and *Clematis viticella* 'Etoile Rose'. The exit from this area leads to the cross axis and then into the white garden, which has a centrepiece of the soft shell-pink hybrid musk rose 'Penelope', *Rosa* 'Schneewittchen', and *Alchemilla mollis*. A *Viburnum* 'Mariesii', with spreading tiers of white hydrangea-like flowers, is planted in each corner.

From the white garden it is easier to go along the canal walk than struggle against the flow of many other visitors back to the path. Then there is a superb view along the main axis, with flowering shrubs lining the path, through the rondel, across the bridge, smothered with *Rosa* 'Veilchenblau', to the tower.

The borders here are richly planted. Yellow tree peonies, calycanthus, and *Enkianthus campanulatum* are underplanted with white-flowered perennials. Nearer to the bridge, the borders are a mixture of pink, blue and white, with *Hydrangea serrata* 'Acuminata Rosalba', cimicifugas, astrantias, and anemones.

The third compartment is the rose garden. There is a superb collection of old roses and in the centre of the garden newer longer-flowering roses have been planted. The fourth compartment is open on one side and there is a bench where you can sit and look over the moat to a pretty private terrace garden.

open: In 1999: 24 May, 25 Jun, 26 Jun, 16 Jul, 17 Jul, 11 Sep, 10am–5pm; dates for the years to come are announced in advance by the Tuinenstichting (see below)

Further information from:
Langbroekerdijk A29,
3947 BR Langbroek
Nederlandse Tuinenstichting:
Tel: (0206) 235 058

Nearby sights of interest:
Hardenbroek; Leeuwenburgh; Kasteel Duurstede and wijk-bij Duurstede.

The medieval tower overlooks a garden of old roses.

open: End May, early Jun, mid-Jul and mid-Oct, Sun, 10am–6pm; telephone for exact days as these vary each year

Further information from:
Mrs Stelling, Wierserallee 9, Vorden
Tel: (0573) 451 409

Nearby sights of interest:
Kasteel Ruurlo; Huis de Voorst; Zutphen: Grote Kerk; Berkelpoort.

A romantic river winds across part of the garden.

31 *De Wiersse*

Location: SE of Apeldoorn, between Zutphen and Ruurlo; take N346 from Zutphen and then N319 towards Vorden and Ruurlo; the entrance to De Wiersse is at 16.7km (10⅓ mile) mark on Zutphen–Winterswijk road; well signed on open days

Several distinct and charming gardens have been laid out around the moated manor house: an 18th-century pleasure garden, a French-style rose garden, an English "sunken garden", and a woodland park. The domain is surrounded by linear features such as canals and lines of beeches. Inside a sinuous river, edged with banks of rhododendrons and azaleas cuts across the site. The combination of classical formality and romantic informality continues throughout the garden.

The park is full of unexpected contrasts, of vistas leading to a statue or to a view outside. There are swamp cypresses, huge beeches, bamboos, and an underplanting of *Maianthemum bifolium*.

The rose garden and the sunken garden were laid out in 1912 by 17-year-old Alice de Stuers, mother of the present owner. They have been renovated but remain in essence much as she designed them. The sunken garden has a central circular pool and fountains with herbaceous borders on three sides and a pergola covered with roses, honeysuckle, and wisteria on the other. It is very beautiful and seems very English. A long tunnel-arbour leads from a circular pool with a waterjet to a secret garden, an enclosed area with old fruit trees.

Erythroniums, camassias, and trilliums flower with the fruit trees and magnolias in early May, followed by rhododendrons and azaleas, dicentras, and trollius. In June clematis, roses, and geraniums bloom. In July the herbaceous borders are at their best and *Primula florindae* grow by the stream edge and waterlilies open in the pools. In October, there is good autumn colour.

open: May to Aug, Sat, 1pm to sunset

Further information from:
Woeziksestraat 473, 6604 CE Wijchen
Tel: (0246) 417 044

Nearby sights of interest:
Nijmegen: Valkhof Park, Grote Markt; De Brinkhof and Kasteel Hernen (see p.53).

32 *Wijchen: Arnoldshof*

Location: 6km (3¾ miles) W of Nijmegen, S of A326 Nijmegen–s'Hertogenbosch road; take exit Beuningen and direction Wijchen; Woeziksestraat is by the first traffic lights and number 473 is on the left

Arnoldshof reveals itself to you slowly. The drive is bordered by Persian lilacs half concealing serious nursery beds and compost heaps. On the left as you near the house suddenly there is a small courtyard garden where peonies, gillenia, dictamnus, and iris all bloom together in a glorious melange. Behind the house is a smooth lawn shaded by three specimen trees, *Liriodendron tulipifera*, *Quercus* x *hispanica* (syn. *Q.* x *lucombeana*), and *Juglans nigra*, and surrounded by herbaceous borders. In the sun, ornamental grasses are planted near the purple-backed leaves of *Ligularia dentata* and cool grey-blue *Amsonia orientalis*. In the shady part of the border *Ribes speciosum*, hostas, and ferns provide the main planting. There is a covetable collection of herbaceous plants, including *Anemone leveillei*, martagon lilies, delphiniums, poppies, hemerocallis, deep red astrantia, and clumps of hostas.

In the central section of the garden a sunken circular pond is paved with brick and surrounded by a pergola planted with vine, wisteria, clematis, honeysuckle, *Akebia quinata*, actinidia, and roses. If the garden ended here, one would feel satisfied at having seen a range of beautifully grown plants in an immaculate design. Yet the most significant part of the garden is still to come.

The Japanese garden is based on gardens of the Heian period (794–1185) and is reached, as it should be, by way of a *roji*, or dewy path. Here, in the place of transition, there is a stone lantern, a water basin which symbolizes purification, and a roofed bench to sit on before entering the quiet and reflective heart of this "stroll garden" created around a lake. The waterfall, frogs, and waterlilies and two small islands are viewed differently from each part of the path. Stepping stones are placed all around the garden across the rocks of the "beaches" and through the ground cover. The islands represent the crane and the turtle, symbols of longevity. All around there are orchids, primulas, and *Iris ensata*.

The *Iris ensata* in the faithfully laid out Japanese garden are at their best in July.

Zeist: Dieptetuin Valkenbosch

Location: From A28/E30 Utrecht–Amersfoort take exit 3, Den Dolder, then bear right into Zeist along Boulevard; at first junction take road directly ahead and second left is Van Tetslaan; the garden is discreetly signed

This small "sunken garden" has a gentle Lutyens and Jekyll atmosphere. Just inside the gate is a rock bank with alpine plants. Herbaceous borders planted with golden rod, daylilies, delphiniums, veronicas, campanulas, and alstromerias surround the sunken lawn with a central pool and fountain. It is well maintained and many of the plants are labelled. Rustic stone steps lead up to pergolas with a wisteria and campsis clambering over and ferns underneath. The garden was designed by C Smitskamp in 1909 for a house which has now disappeared. There is, unfortunately, an insensitive modern replacement.

open: Mar to Oct, 8am to sunset

Further information from: Van Tetslaan, Zeist

Nearby sights of interest: Nearby Slot Zeist is a cultural centre with a restaurant in the basement that incorporates a shell grotto designed by Daniel Marot; interesting private garden at Lyceumlaan 6, 3707 EC Zeist, M Diepeveen, tel: (0306) 924 837 and fax: (0306) 924 047

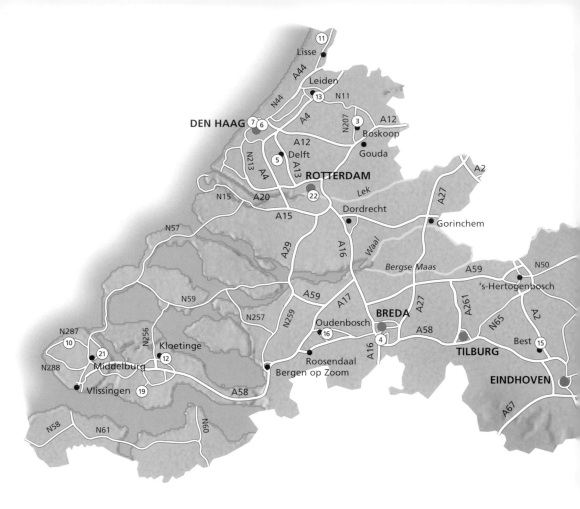

Key to gardens

1 **Kasteeltuinen Arcen**
2 **Kasteel Baexem**
3 **Proefstation, Boskoop**
4 **Kasteel Bouvigne**
5 **Cultuurtuin, Botanische Tuin, Delft**
6 **Clingendael**
7 **Westbroekpark**
8 **Han Njio Tuin**

9 **Huys de Dohm**
10 **De Kempenhof**
11 **De Keukenhof**
12 **Lenshoek Tuin**
13 **Hortus Botanicus, Leiden**
14 **De Heerenhof**
15 **Odulphushof Botanische Tuinen**
16 **Arboretum Oudenbosch**

17 **D'n Hof Botanische Tuin**
18 **De Rhulenhof Kwekerij and Tuinen**
19 **Slot de Nisse**
20 **Botanische Tuin Jochum-Hof**
21 **De Tintelhof**
22 **Arboretum Trompenburg**

Key

══════ Motorways
══════ Principal trunk highways
③ Gardens
⬤ Major towns and cities
• Towns

Southern Netherlands

The four provinces included in Southern Netherlands are unusually varied. In Zuid-Holland, the capital of the Netherlands, The Hague (Den Haag or 's-Gravenhage) with its galleries, museums, and shops, together with the industrial city and port of Rotterdam are part of the southern loop of the Randstad or "Ring City". North of this loop of built-up land is the "Green Heart", an area of farmland and intensive horticulture, which includes the historic cities of Leiden and Gouda, as well as the bulb fields and displays at De Keukenhof (see p.86). The flat landscape of *bollenstreek* or "bulb-strip" is scattered in spring with squares of brilliant colour. The soil is spectacularly rich and the nursery centre of Boskoop (see pp.80–1), criss-crossed with dykes, is worth visiting.

Zeeland is a province of reclaimed land, dotted with small towns and villages, and until the Delta Project was finished in 1986 always at risk of severe flooding. The Delta Project dammed the estuaries of the Rhine, the Maas, and the Schelde protecting the islands of Zuid-Holland and Zeeland. There are some fine buildings in Middelburg, the largest town in the province,

Roses contrast with clipped yew at Kasteel Bouvigne.

The Arboretum Trompenburg contains a magnificent collection of conifers.

although Veere, a tiny harbour town, is possibly even more attractive. There are many excellent gardens here but they are private and only open on certain weekends or by appointment (see pages 85, 86, 91, and 92), so a visit to see them needs advance planning. Only the native plant garden attached to the Botanic Museum at Kasteel Westhoeve is open regularly.

North Brabant extends from the inlets of the North Sea almost to the German border and is the second largest province in the Netherlands. The province consists mainly of sandy heathland like that found in Northern Flanders, and is bordered on the north and east by the River Maas. There are many areas of attractive woodland, such as Landgoed Lievensberg near Bergen op Zoom, as well as an industrialized area around Eindhoven. The towns of Breda with the castle and herb garden at the Begijnhof (see p.81) and the capital, 's-Hertogenbosch (Den Bosch), are definitely worth exploring.

The rose trials at Westbroekpark in The Hague.

The province of Limburg is long and narrow, stretching along the German border from Gelderland in the north to the province of Liège in Belgium in the south. The capital Maastricht is one of the oldest towns in the country, a crossroads between Germany, Belgium, and the Netherlands. It is lively and beautiful, with two fine Romanesque churches, pretty squares, and ancient town walls. In Limburg there are exciting gardens such as De Heerenhof (see p.88), Kasteel Baexem (see p.80), and those of designers Ineke Greve at Huys de Dohm (see pp.84–5) and Han Njio (see p.84). Other gardens to see are at Kasteel Mheer, Kasteel Eijsden, and Kasteel Neercanne, which is now a hotel with a steeply terraced garden.

Exquisite contrasts of shape, texture, and colour make Han Njio's garden very special.

At impeccable Huys de Dohm the zig-zag hedge is of hornbeam and the ground cover is *Tiarella cordifolia*.

Kasteeltuinen Arcen

Location: On German border, S of Nijmegen, E of Eindhoven, and just N of Venlo; exit to Kasteeltuinen Arcen clearly signed on the N271 Venlo to Nijmegen road

open: 28 Mar to 30 Sep, daily, 10am–6pm; Oct, daily, 11am–5pm

Further information from:
Lingsforterweg 26, Arcen
Tel: (077) 473 1882
Fax: (077) 473 2501

Nearby sights of interest:
Venlo: Stadhuis, St Martinuskerk.

Kasteel Arcen dates back to the 17th century and was completely restored in 1988. The large complex of exhibition gardens was created at the same time and was designed to attract and absorb a considerable number of visitors, adults and children.

The central section of the garden consists of three moated islands. The castle, with an additional moat, and the outbuildings, now a restaurant, pottery, and orangery where plants are for sale, are on the first island. As you cross the moat to the second island, there is a tunnel-arbour or *berceau* and steps up to a viewing platform from where there is a bird's eye view of the surroundings. The second island is rose island, where ten rose

The Thai house overlooks a pool full of koi carp.

The tree-covered walk is shady in summer.

This theme garden has a metal
grid walkway across the pool.

The central water feature
is bold and dramatic.

Patterns of brick contrast
with pebbles along the
alchemilla-fringed path.

Miniature roses and white violas
in bloom around a circular pond.

gardens in different styles are laid out round a Baroque pool and
shell-shaped waterfall. A garden of climbing roses adjoins an
aviary full of brightly coloured parrots. An angular black iron
pergola with tiny pyramidal roofs supports the roses. There is a
garden of miniature roses and a romantic garden of old roses
underplanted with geraniums and violas, somewhat spoiled by
the addition of begonias and sentimental statues. A classic rose
garden of old roses interspersed with peonies is followed by
another romantic garden with climbers twined round obelisks.
In all there are 20,000 roses.

Near a hosta garden a large stylized figure of a cat sits on top
of a concrete tree trunk overlooking the bridge to the third
island, the Sparrenbos or pine wood. From a viewing platform a
decked walk leads through a dark pine forest, where chickens,
deer, art works, and Vietnamese pot-bellied pigs share the
muddy forest floor.

After leaving the three islands, a path continues under a
brick arch, built aslant to symbolize the change from the old
castle garden to the new, to the Lommerick or shady, foliage
garden. Angular paths made of geometric slabs zig-zag between
bold foliage planting and there are collections of astilbes, iris,
and hemerocallis and, in places, a light canopy of small trees.
It is a lively piece of modern landscaping.

After that comes the vast glasshouse, the Casa Verde, where
tender plants grow: callistemons, albizzia, palms, a huge and
ancient fig, and many other tropical and subtropical trees. The
journey through the Casa Verde is accompanied by the sound of

running water from waterfalls and streams edged with arums and strelitzias. There are areas with different temperatures and very different atmospheres. One section with subtle grey planting is enlivened by a dramatic toucan. Pots of agaves, kalanochoes, and hibiscus are scattered everywhere. Enormous hanging baskets of vivid geraniums, a row of ligustrum, and tubs of datura and oleander add to the exotic effect. There is a café here with a large deck overlooking a lake.

A series of small model gardens follows: a Chinese garden, a flower garden, and an innovative water garden where metal grids make footpaths over the water but still allow the water plants to flourish and even grow through the mesh. The gardens of grasses, topiary, and alpine plants, in particular, are full of ideas for owners of small gardens. The area is full of startling contrasts. A conventional rock garden with raised beds and troughs is close to the "Avant-garden" with its aluminium floor, mirrored obelisk, and a planting of vibrant orange and pink poppies. Nearby there is a return to traditional gardening with a collection of irises.

The scale of the landscape then changes dramatically. Tall eremurus grow on an area of giant scree and a "canyon" said to be over 1,000m (3,300ft) long has been created with gigantic pieces of rock. Troughs of rock plants have been sited here. Walk through the canyon to the Eastern garden with its bamboo bridges, tea-houses, and acer collection. The balcony of a Thai house overlooks numerous ponds filled with koi carp and even rice fields. The eastern theme is continued with a bamboo walk, a cherry tree garden, and a Japanese maple garden.

The modern glasshouse is sited by a large lake.

A statue of Buddha looks over the pool in the Eastern garden.

open: All year, daily except
Mon, 11am–5pm

Further information from:
Kasteelweg 7, 6095 ND Baexem
Tel: (0475) 452 843

Nearby sights of interest:
Roermond: Munsterkerk
and cathedral.

**A battered giant rises from
the grotto.**

Kasteel Baexem

Location: About 8km (5 miles) W of Roermond on N280 to Weert; cross N273 at
Haelen and on reaching Baexem take the left turn direction Grathem and the castle
is immediately on the left

This exhilarating garden is quite unlike any other in Holland.
Plant names are painted on stones. Cambered roof tiles are piled
up to make a protecting arc behind a curved seat. A circle of
fastigiate poplars invaded by oaks, honeysuckles, and rambler
roses is lined by a crescent of stacked logs. Another enclosed
circle is contrived entirely from a giant grass. A raised brick
terrace is shaded by flat parasols of trained standard willows.
Whereas the Jardins de la Fontaine at Nîmes are like a giant,
stone sunken parterre, at Baexem there are also strange sunken
streams, a grotto, and a sprawling grotesque figure but the scale
is tiny. There is no geometry and no stone, and it is the bricks
and curves that make something entirely original.

Most of the plants are chosen to attract birds, butterflies, and
bees. In early summer there are geraniums and standard roses,
later pear trees, fastigiate elm, buddleja, thyme, and rosebay
willow herb all flourish in a glorious high summer jumble.
Numerous fruit trees in the garden add to its luxuriant air. There
are many good trees, including a liquidambar, a big golden
robinia, and a group of three unusually large contorted willows.

---

open: All year, Mon to Fri,
8.30am–5pm

Further information from:
Rijneveld 153, 2771 XV Boskoop
Tel: (0172) 219 797
Fax: (0172) 219 717

Nearby sights of interest:
Boskoop: Boomkwekerij and
Rosarium; Gouda: Stadhuis,
St Janskerk, and Waaghuis.

Boskoop: Proefstation

Location: Boskoop is 30km (18½ miles) E of The Hague and W of Utrecht; leave
A12/E30 at Knooppunt Gouwe, near Gouda, and take N207 to Boskoop, follow
directions to VVV and take second on left beyond it, continue down Goudserijweg
and at the bottom turn right to Rijneveld

Boskoop is a name familiar to most gardeners for the town, the
centre of the Dutch nursery industry, has given its name to a
variety of cultivars ranging from blackcurrants to conifers. The
Proefstation is the trial ground for ornamental plants, many bred
in the region such as *Cytisus* 'Boskoop Ruby' and *Hemerocallis*
'Dutch Beauty'. There is a large collection of well-labelled plants,
many laid out in an attractive way. These trial grounds are always
changing, and while some beds look well clothed and established,
others look like nursery beds. However, for the serious gardener
and flower lover the Proefstation is totally absorbing.

The beds are laid out on a long narrow site between three
canals and while there are some which contain all the cultivars or
species of one subject being trialled, this is not always the case.

A small tree such as *Cercis canadensis* 'Forest Pansy' is grouped with *Cytisus decumbens* and *Stachys* 'Silver Carpet' for visual effect, while nearby is a collection of mahonias, including *Mahonia aquifolium* 'Green Ripple' and *M. a.* 'Donewell' with narrower twisted leaves and no berries, planted so that their differences can be observed.

All the plants are grown without fungicides or insecticides. The strongest cultivars are selected and those which succumb to disease are discarded. This is particularly so in the rose garden. Belgian rose breeder, Louis Lens, has a white rose named after his wife, *Rosa* 'Maria Matilda' (syn. 'Lenmar') seen in all the best Dutch and Belgian gardens, and this has proved very resistant to black spot. Other resistant roses include *R.* 'Bonica', *R.* 'The Fairy', and *R.* 'Interleer'. Methods of gardening are trialled too. Tagetes are grown in blocks close to other plants to keep the soil free from pests. A ground-cover plant which has been successful and kept ground weed-free for five years is a mildew free aster, *Aster ageratoides* 'Astran' (syn. *A. trinervius ageratoides*).

 # *Kasteel Bouvigne*

Location: S of city centre; come off motorway A16/E19 exit 15, Rijsbergen, and follow signs to the Mastbos; Kasteel Bouvigne is signed in yellow

open: All year, Mon to Fri, 8.30am–4pm

Further information from:
Bouvignelaan 5, 4800 CE Breda
Tel: (076) 564 1000

Nearby sights of interest:
Begijnhof with Kruidtuin, Park Valkenberg; Grote Kerk.

Kasteel Bouvigne dates from the early 17th century and is in a typical Brabantine style, of brick and stone and with crisp black and white painted shutters. The castle rises straight out of a lake surrounded by rhododendrons and overlooked by a small oriental pavilion which adds to the romantic atmosphere.

There is an air of the municipal park about these formal gardens. The horticulture is of a high standard and the grounds are very well maintained. A formal French garden, a symmetrical

Summer bedding under rose arches.

layout of box-edged beds filled with roses, is designed round a central statue of cherubs supporting an urn. There is a long palissade of thuja with statues in niches and clumps of bright bamboo, instead of the usual box, trimmed into dome shapes. In front is a large rectangular pond with a prostrate conifer softening one corner of it. The area is surrounded by climbing roses and there are broad walks lined by imposing cylindrical yews.

open: All year, Mon to Fri
8.30am–5pm and Sat 10am–3pm

Further information from:
Julianalaan 67, 2628 BC Delft
Tel: (015) 278 2356

Nearby sights of interest:
Old Delft, Oostpoort, Niewe Kerk,
canals (singels).

Inside the glasshouse.

5 *Delft: Cultuurtuin Botanische Tuin*

Location: On the outskirts of Delft, just outside the Oostendepoort; from A13/E19 take exit 9, Delft, and turn left just before Oostende gate (signed to Naaldwijk and Royal Delft) into Julianalaan; park in nearby residential area

This modestly sized botanic garden was started in 1917. It is separated into three parts by the greenhouses. They are extensive and contain many tropical and subtropical plants, in particular special collections of bananas, gingers, and Marantaceae, which are similar to the gingers but from America.

Cannas, hedychiums, bay trees, and other Mediterranean plants in pots are taken from the orangery and lined up alongside the main path in the summer.

There is a collection of witch hazels in the middle garden as well as two large metasequoias, a *Paliurus spina-christi*, one of the trees believed to have been used in the crown of thorns, and *Zanthoxylum simulans*, another spiny tree.

There is a rock garden, a garden of herbaceous plants, and a garden of native plants. This has a narrow stream with boggy margins where marsh marigolds grow. The homeopathic garden contains native plants like the foxglove, *Digitalis purpurea*, while the garden of plants with aromatic oils includes lavender, *Rosa gallica*, *R. pomifera*, *Anthemis tinctoria*, and *Vitex agnus castus*.

---

open: All year, daily, sunrise to sunset; Japanese garden: May to mid-Jun

Further information from:
Wassenaarseweg, Den Haag
Tel: (070) 353 5856

Nearby sights of interest:
Huis ten Bosch; Binnenhof;
Mauritshuis; Ridderzaal;
Noordeinde Palace.

6 *Den Haag: Clingendael*

Location: Continue to end of A12 and turn right onto N44 towards Wassenaar, after 1km (¾ mile) turn left into Clingendael laan

The original 17th-century garden at Clingendael was one of the earliest French-style formal gardens to be constructed in the Netherlands. It was designed by Philips Doublet, the owner, who was married to the daughter of Constantijn Huygens. Doublet travelled often to France to see the gardens of André Le Nôtre but the flatness of the site, the surrounding canals, and the elongated plots gave a new Dutch character to his finished design. All this has gone, although there are plans for carrying out restoration work.

Today the garden is largely a landscape park with expanses of grass, winding canals, serpentine lakes, and many trees. Within the boundaries are a Japanese garden, a rhododendron wood, a rose garden, and an old Dutch garden situated near a 17th-century stairway believed to have been designed by Daniel Marot.

The jewel of the garden today is the Japanese garden. In 1895 the owner of Clingendael, the Baroness van Brienen, visited Japan and was so impressed by the gardens she saw that she brought back rocks, bridges, lanterns, and even a complete tea-house. The resulting garden, a reconstruction of a tea-garden in a style which was fashionable in Japan between 1580 and 1630, is exquisite. It is believed that the Baroness designed the garden herself. Near the entrance there is a mound with a stone lantern on it, and another just beyond, to light the way to the tea-house. Finely cut Japanese acers, ferns, and bamboo make delicate contrasts at the edge of the meandering stream which represents the course of life, beginning in the east, where the sun rises, and with bends and stones that symbolize difficulties. The final destination of the water is hidden, as is the future.

The red tea-house is the centre of garden. From here you can gaze over the pool at the Guardian stone and at the stone which resembles a turtle and represents long life. All the stones in the garden have particular meanings.

The Baroness would only allow four people at a time into the garden, as more would disturb its spirits. Today it is only open for six weeks of the year when the azaleas are in flower and the acers in fresh leaf. At weekends visitors shuffle round toe to heel. Try to visit the garden on a weekday when it is quiet, and the symbolism and tranquillity can be fully appreciated.

The tea-house and the stones came from Japan at the end of the 19th century.

7 *Den Haag: Westbroekpark*

Location: In The Hague, follow signs for Madurodam and continue towards Scheveningen for about 500m (⅓ mile)

open: All year, daily, sunrise to sunset; Rosarium: until end Oct

This public park in the English landscape style is The Hague's centre of horticultural excellence and is definitely worth visiting. It is well planted and immaculately maintained. There are large irregular lawns surrounded by extensive shrub borders, sheltered by mature trees.

The rose garden is now the venue for the annual rose competition when each year, rose growers from all over the world send in their newest roses for trials. The best ones are given certificates which allows them to compete for the title "Golden Rose of the city of The Hague".

There are varied and interesting sculptures in the garden and, in the summer, well-chosen and well-grown tender plants are bedded out. Crab apples and berrying shrubs extend the colour until well into the autumn.

Further information from:
Kapelweg, Scheveningen
Tel: (070) 353 5676

Nearby sights of interest:
Kuurhaus, Scheveningen; Madurodam; Kasteel Duivenvoorde, Museum Constantijn Huygens at Hofwyck.

open: 29 May to 5 Jul, every weekend, 10am–6pm

Further information from:
't Blauwe, Gasthuis 14,
6268 NN Bemelen
Tel: (043) 407 8007

Nearby sights of interest:
Maastricht; ruins of Kasteel Valkenburg.

8 *Han Njio Tuin*

Location: From Maastricht follow directions for either Berg en Terblijt or Valkenburg, then look for signs for Bemelen; in Bemelen go straight on up the hill and the blue house is on the right after some distance

Designer Han Njio's garden is a fascinating combination of classical, oriental, Mediterranean, and cottage garden features.

Much attention is paid to the composition of foliage; the colour, shape, and texture of a plant's leaves must enhance those of its neighbour. Proportion too is important in this garden. Awkward corners are disguised with subtle planting. Most trees in the garden are small and lightly foliaged, and heavier looking maples are trained to keep them to scale. There are vistas from one section to another, perhaps down a small avenue or through the contrasting leaves of bamboo and petasites to a fountain.

Among the many unusual plant groupings, an arrangement of standard *Colutea arborescens* makes a striking composition. These mopheaded trees have trunks which are delightfully wonky and they are echoed by another bladder senna, not far away, which grows as it will. In evidence in the garden are finely cut leaves and foamy flowers, delicate and insubstantial and at the same softly coloured, such as a late-flowering elder and tamarisk.

---

open: First three weekends in Jun, 10am–5pm

Further information from:
de Dohm 50, 6419 CX Heerlen
Tel: (045) 571 0470

Morning glories over an arch.

9 *Huys de Dohm*

Location: E of Maastricht; from N281 from N (Roermond/Geleen) take exit Heerlen Zuid/Ziekenhuis, turn right to Welten, then second right and first left; from A76 to Heerlen take exit 7, Heerlen Centrum, and take first right, John F Kennedylaan; after 2km (¼ mile) turn left into Tichelbeekstraat and Huys de Dohm is on the left

The front of Huys de Dohm dates from 1640 and has a dignified formal garden: a lawn with a square of trained limes and ivy, topiary, fountains, a wall, and seats.

Ineke Greve's outstanding 2.5ha (6 acre) garden comprises about ten different rooms, separated by tall hedges. The first section is the long double border. Billowing herbaceous plants such as phlox, lilies, astrantias, and geraniums in soft pinks, mauves, and purples are lifted from the commonplace by the introduction of rich, dull-red nicotiana and *Persicaria amplexicaulis*.

In the rose garden, topiary shapes add form and give winter interest. Then comes the white garden with a pretty trellis pavilion at one end. A downy camomile lawn is surrounded by gravel paths and borders of *Clematis viticella* 'Alba Luxurians', *Aster divaricatus*, violas, roses, astrantia, lilies, cosmos, and nicotiana.

The quiet garden is the still centre of Huys de Dohm. The lawn is divided into four squares and enclosed by high hedges. Here there is only green, an intricate piece of box *broderie* and two young walnut trees. The maple walk, behind the quiet garden, is planted with spring bulbs and is part of the cross axis from one side of the garden to the other.

There is a vegetable and herb garden with four standard roses in the centre surrounded by an inner ring of rhubarb and then some spectacular cabbages with long crumpled blue-green leaves. The flame garden is a fantastic cheering melange of orange lilies, 'Bishop of Llandaff' dahlias, *Crocosmia* 'Lucifer', frilly purple basil, and *Scabious atropurpurea*. Almost finally, the water garden is planted with clear blue and yellow flowers: lime-yellow nicotiana, metallic-blue cerinthe, *Salvia patens*, and the soft yellow *Anthemis* 'E C Buxton'.

De Kempenhof

Location: Coming from Middelburg, follow signs to Oostkapelle and Domburg; Zuiverseweg is on the left just before the village of Domburg

open: First weekend in Jul and by appointment

Further information from:
Zuiverseweg 4, Domburg
Tel: (011) 858 1647

Nearby sights of interest:
Westhove Kasteel and Biologische Museum, tel: (011) 858 2620.

Geraniums in the woodland garden.

It is difficult to believe but "De Kempenhof" was a flat onion field before it was developed into the glorious garden it is today. The first thing Madeleine van Bennekom had to do when she started the garden 33 years ago, was to plant a shelterbelt to protect the site from salt winds off the North Sea.

The garden is structured near the house and becomes less formal as you move away into the surrounding woodland. The flowering year begins in the meadow garden with snowflakes, primula, and daffodils and continues with bluebells and geraniums until July when the site is cut. Another memorable area is the woodland garden. Under tall conifers and deciduous trees, there is a succession of wildflowers like buttercups and garden flowers such as geraniums and more unusual plants. A collection of hellebores is another feature of the garden in early spring.

This is a wonderful garden in which to learn about placing plants in effective combinations, such as the shrub *Neillia thibetica* with an underplanting of *Dicentra* 'Bacchanal'. A border of grasses is carefully interspersed with other plants, such as ferns, to avoid too much uniformity. The herbaceous border has a background of golden yew hedge and behind that are striking dark green domed columns of yew, another golden dome, and then the varied leaves of the trees in the shelterbelt. Another eye-catching feature are the clipped hawthorns, standard *Crataegus laevigata* 'Paul's Scarlet' which emerge like large lollipops behind a cypress hedge and echo a grove of alliums across the drive.

 open: 25 Mar to 19 May and 19 Aug to 19 Sep, daily, 8am–7.30pm

Further information from:
PO Box 66, 2160 AB Lisse
Tel: (0252) 465 5555

Nearby sights of interest:
Bollenstreek (tulip fields).

The famous tulip beds.

11 *De Keukenhof*

Location: Lisse is between Haarlem and Leiden on N208, Keukenhof is well signed

The landscape park of De Keukenhof was acquired in 1949 by the Royal Dutch Association of Bulb Growers, who wished to provide an attractive setting in which to display their products. The park had been laid out by J D Zocher the younger in 1854, and there are woodland glades, meandering streams, and avenues of beeches. In this attractive setting, the area has been divided into many different plots and the bulb growers take part in a ballot each year to determine which of them they can have. The park is open for two months each year, and during that period blocks and strips of flowering bulbs in every possible place dazzle and enthral the visitors who arrive in their thousands.

It is a brilliant spectacle and not confined to tulips. In the early part of the year there are narcissi and these are followed by crocus, muscari, fritillaries, including ranks of imposing crown imperials, hyacinths, lilies, and alstroemerias. In addition there are 5,000 sq m (50,000 sq ft) of glasshouse, where again you will find blocks of tulips and some other flowers. Tulips are the queens of Keukenhof and here and outside you will find cultivars you have never seen before, with luscious colours and enchanting feathering or fringed edges. As this is a commercial exhibition you can order bulbs for the following year.

 open: Jun, by appointment only

Further information from:
Marktveld 19, Kloetinge
Tel: (0113) 215 116

Nearby sights of interest:
Goes: Grote Kerk.

12 *Kloetinge: Lenshoek Tuin*

Location: From A58/E312 motorway Vlissingen–Bergen op Zoom, take exit 35 to 's-Gravenpolder and then direction Kloetinge; Marktveld is the square adjacent to the parish church in Kloetinge

This garden comes as a complete surprise. The miniature landscape park that you first see on entering the garden is unique in Zeeland, as are the huge oaks, beeches, a massive *Sequoiadendron giganteum*, a *Pterocarya fraxinifolia*, and a maple that is listed as a "national monument". A bridge over a stream leads into the second part of the garden, an artificial mound. A symphoricarpos and philadelphus walk was planted by the owner's grandfather and is very characteristic of the 1920s when the snow berries were the latest fashion.

Beyond the mound the garden reverts to Zeeland flatness. There are beds of flowers under ancient quince and medlar trees with wonderfully contorted trunks. At right angles, long rectangular beds are arranged along a central axis leading to a bench. This is where the old rose borders are, the pink and white roses chosen for their scent. Here you can find *Aesculus parviflora* with geraniums growing underneath, many different peonies, and herbaceous plants such as *Anemone aconitifolium*, *Knautia macedonica*, *Geranium nodosum*, and a collection of irises. At the end of the central vista, the path turns back towards the house, past a hellebore border, a *Magnolia soulangeana*, and several massive rhododendrons.

13 *Leiden: Hortus Botanicus*

Location: In the centre of Leiden, not far from St Peter's Church; cars should park at Parking Molen de Valk or Parking Haagweg, then 15 minutes walk

The famous botanist Carolus Clusius (Charles de l'Ecluse) was founder, designer, and first Prefect of the Botanic Garden in 1594. Earlier in his career Clusius had introduced many new plants into northern Europe from Turkey, in particular tulips, hyacinths, crown imperials, lilies, narcissi, and ranunculus. He can be said to be the founder of the Dutch bulb industry.

The reconstruction of that original Leiden Botanic Garden of 1594, the Hortus Clusius, is today one of the most delightful parts of the garden. Paths of white crushed shells outline brick-edged narrow rectangular beds planted with those early tulips with the date of introduction on each label.

Although the botanic garden today is a centre for serious botanical studies the ordinary gardener cannot fail to enjoy a large border of herbaceous plants, planted for colour and form, and a rose garden which was laid out in the 1930s. A central sundial is surrounded by those species from which all cultivars descend: *Rosa alba*, *R. centifolia*, *R. damascena*, and *R. gallica*.

The Von Siebold Memorial Garden is another special garden within the garden. Siebold is a name familiar from plants such as clematis and *Hosta sieboldii*. There are many other introductions, like wisteria, tiarella, and epimediums. Von Siebold was a doctor working in Japan in 1823 and sent back most of his plant collection to Leiden. A Japanese garden of raked gravel, rocks, and bamboo was created in his memory in 1990.

The greenhouses have some splendid collections of plants, including Aristolochia and Cycads. Summer visitors should not miss seeing the 65 different passion flowers. A lengthy corridor is planted with passion flowers, stephanotis, and *Aristolochia grandiflora* – the stink plant. The collection of semi-tender trees in tubs, such as olives and pittosporum, dating from the 17th century, are moved outside in summer from the orangery designed by Daniel Marot.

open: 1 Apr to 30 Sep, Mon to Sat, 9am–5pm; 1 Oct to 31 Mar, Mon to Fri, 9am–5pm; Clusius Garden: all year, Mon to Fri, 9–5pm; greenhouses: close at 4.30pm; closes 3 Oct, and 25 Dec to 2 Jan

Further information from:
Rapenburg 73, Leiden
Tel: (071) 527 5144

Nearby sights of interest:
The old town of Leiden and its museums.

The 16th-century Hortus Clusius restored to the original plan.

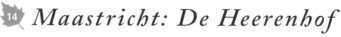

14 *Maastricht: De Heerenhof*

open: Third weekend, Sun only, in Mar (for Hellebores), 10am–5pm; first, second, and third weekend Jun and first weekend Jul, 10am–5pm

Further information from:
Veldstraat 12a,
6227 SZ Maastricht
Tel: (043) 361 6267

Nearby sights of interest:
Kasteel Neercanne; Kasteel Eijsden; Maastricht: old town, churches, and Bonnefanten Museum.

Location: From A2/E25 Heerlen–Liuk/Liège motorway follow the signs for MECC and Academic Ziekenhuis (Hospital); turn left and at the end of the road turn left again, then first right at the roundabout and 12a is on the right

The approach is not promising, for the front of De Heerenhof lies directly on an unattractive road on the outskirts of Maastricht. However, this is an area where the town comes to an abrupt halt and behind the house is a surprisingly long, narrow garden that encompasses many styles from elegant terrace to tiny smallholding.

Immediately behind the house, pots are filled with pale blue *Plumbago auriculata* and creamy-yellow nasturtiums. Then there is a raised gravel terrace, edged with brick and shaded by a paulownia and planted with hostas. Further along a curving hedge of lavender draws the visitor down the garden.

From here on revelations begin. There are borders and areas of amazing richness contrasted with cool geometry, high gardening with ecological *laissez-faire*, and wild grasses with giant dahlias.

A wonderful, glowing mid- to late summer border consisted of *Clematis heraclifolia*, purply-blue monk's hood, purple erigerons, magenta bergamot, deep pink phlox, delicate-stemmed *Verbena bonariensis* against a background of rusty-rose *Persicaria amplexicaulis*, orange kniphofias, and the apricot-coloured *Buddleja weyeriana*. Then there is the natural water garden. From a bench on another raised terrace one can look over the pond with the small bridges, rushes, and water plants and observe the wildlife.

Huge round heads of crimson dahlias echo the fading alliums in the dahlia garden at the end of De Heerenhof.

After this natural area, there is a path with clustered spheres of box on one side which leads to a double ring of pleached limes inside a circle of box, an area where all is controlled and restricted – the antithesis of the water garden before and the flower gardens beyond. In a flower garden there is a resplendent mixture of roses the colour of cardinal's robes, anemones, purple sage, purple-leaved cannas, and scarlet dahlias.

Almost at the end is the dahlia garden. Nasturtiums, vast dahlias in apricots, mauve, and scarlet mixed with fading alliums, and the odd red cabbage are all kept in order by narrow box hedges. The garden ends in a crescendo of brilliant colour. Except of course for the last enclosure where hens freely range, the final contrast.

Odulphushof Botanische Tuinen

Location: Best is 11km (7 miles) W of Eindhoven; take A2/E25 to 's-Hertogenbosch (Den Bosch) then exit 28, Best; the garden is behind the church of St Odulphus

open: Apr to Sep, Sun and Feast Days, 1–5pm

Further information from:
Kerkhofpad 5, Best
Tel: (0499) 371 295

Nearby sights of interest:
Kasteel Heeswijk, SE of Den Bosch; Den Bosch: museum and churches.

Rust-tinged stones edge the borders and make mounds and walls for growing the 2,000 hardy plants in this small, botanic garden. There is a varied collection of wild and cultivated plants, and also a number of fruit trees and bushes, so there are rather charming combinations such as *Nagelkruid* (everything is labelled only in Dutch) or *Geum rivale*, hostas, and the giant butterbur or *Groot Hoefblad* beneath ancient apple trees, like 'Early Victoria' and 'Gravensteyn'. Underneath an old mulberry are Jerusalem artichokes, a vine, and some daylilies.

Exotic trees and native flowers.

Loganberries, apricots, and figs grow against the church walls. The Priest's House is next to the church and makes a right angle with it where there is a long lawn with a Himalayan cedar, a weeping ash, and some flowers. One sunny patch contains a collection of irises, including the bearded *Iris* 'Colley's Baccarat', *I.* 'Colley's Marie Philips', and *I. tectorum*.

The fruit and paths and the main show garden have been restored in recent years. In 1980 the garden in its new form was opened by Prince Claus who planted a *Ginkgo biloba*.

Arboretum Oudenbosch

Location: Oudenbosch is N of Roosendaal; take exit 22, Oudenbosch, from A17 Roosendaal–Dordrecht road; immediately after the Basilica in Oudenbosch and close to the railway station

open: 1 Apr to 31 Oct, Sun, 1–5pm; 1 May to end Aug, in addition, Tue to Fri, 1.30–4pm

Further information from:
Ankerstraat, 4731 Oudenbosch
Tel: (0165) 315 008

Nearby sights of interest:
Basilica at Oudenbosch.

This attractive arboretum is maintained and run by volunteers, with the help of donations from local nurserymen and money from local sponsors. It is still expanding, with new areas of planting being added. In the more established areas, one magnificent weeping beech must be 24m (80ft) across and there are collections of viburnums, calycanthas, and aesculus.

There is far more colour than is usual in an arboretum. The older established areas are underplanted with wildflowers, hostas, and many flowering shrubs such as *Paeonia suffruticosa*, *Spiraea japonica* 'Bullata', *Neillia thibetica*, and heathers. Additional colour comes in summer from clumps of glowing blue *Iris sibirica*, *Azalea mollis*, and blood red poppies. There is a *heemtuin* by the long pool, a large area of Asiatic plants, a small Zen garden, and an unusual feature for an arboretum, a huge false stone "grotto".

17 *Overloon: D'n Hof Botanische Tuin*

open: 1 Mar to 31 Oct, Mon to Sat 9.30am–5pm and Sun and Public Holidays 11am–6pm

Further information from:
Stevensbeekseweg 19–21,
5825 ZG Overloon
Tel: (0478) 642 761

Nearby sights of interest:
Kasteel Helmond Museum;
's-Hertogenbosch: St Jean's Cathedral; North Brabant Museum.

Location: About 30km (18½ miles) S of Nijmegen; take A73/E31 direction Venlo, then exit 7 Vierlingsbeek, direction Overloon; D'n Hof is outside the village in direction of Stevensbeek

This remote botanic garden has recently been taken over by a different authority and may well lose its air of being forgotten by time. It is well looked after and there is an extensive collection of trees. However they are not labelled, except for seven common trees planted round a heather garden with a central pond.

Near the entrance there are raised beds followed by a large lawn decorated with palms, agaves, and cycads in tubs. In addition to the tree and shrub collection, there are rock gardens large and small, planted with conifers and native plants, order beds containing members of the lily family, a herb garden, and a patch of meadowland with lupins and local wildflowers.

18 *De Rhulenhof Kwekerij and Tuinen*

open: 15 May to 1 Oct, Tue to Sat 10am–5pm and Sun 1–5pm; nursery: last week in Mar to 1 Oct, Tue to Sat, 10am–5pm and from 15 May, also on Sun, 1–5pm

Further information from:
Kleefseweg 14, Ottersum,
gem Gennep
Tel: (0485) 518 039

Nearby sights of interest:
Nijmegen: Waag.

The circular pool in the rose garden.

Location: Gennep is 20km (12½ miles) S of Nijmegen on the N271 to Venlo; close by Gennep follow signs Gennep/Ottersum/Kleef; continue through Ottersum towards Ven-Zelderheide and De Rhulenhof is on the right

The first part of this garden is of rooms enclosed by tall yew hedges surrounding the original farmhouse. Among the rooms are one with flower borders and in another, a classically restrained pool garden with four bold symmetrical pillars at each corner covered with *Wisteria floribunda* 'Macrobotrys'.

In the rose garden there are many exquisite old roses and a small *bassin* surrounded by lavender and clipped box. Then there are steps up to a higher garden. Roses grow over two arches and climb up metal posts arranged as triangular obelisks.

Near the house is a courtyard with pots of tender plants, such as cistus and brugmansias. Running the whole length of one side of the site is a pear avenue with an open-sided domed pavilion in the centre, double borders of shrubs and herbaceous plants, and a central bed consisting of globes of box and acaena. At the back of the house, around the lake, is a natural area of open land. Behind that is a new modern layout for a subtropical container garden. This will soon be joined by a conservatory with more tropical plants, offering further delights for the flower lover.

Slot de Nisse

Location: Nisse is S of Goes; leave A58/E312 motorway at exit 35 and take direction 's-Gravenpolder, after about 4km (2½ miles) Nisse is signed to the W; Slot de Nisse is behind the church in the village centre

open: First weekend in Jul; also by appointment

Further information from:
Dorpsplein 25, Nisse
Tel: (0113) 649 469

Nearby sights of interest:
Foundations of Kasteel Hellenburg; Kwekerij Eleonore de Koning; Eleonore De Koning Kwekerij Van Vaste Planten (herbaceous plant nursery), Kruipuitsedijk 3, 4436 RC Oudelande, tel: (0113) 548 634 and fax: (0113) 548 389.

Slot de Nisse is by the church and the village green. It is part a garden of quite formal "rooms", divided by hedges of hornbeam, box, and privet, and part a country garden with a pond and sections that extend into the surrounding fields.

To the left of the gate in a sunny area are superb double borders of softly coloured herbaceous plants combined with rounded bushes of *Syringa microphylla*, peonies, alliums, and old roses. Close by there is a pergola with pear trees and clematis underplanted with epimediums, *Omphalodes cappadocica*, and hostas. There are mounds of *Hydrangea petiolaris* used refreshingly as ground cover at one end and a stone seat at the other. It is enclosed and shady, a complete contrast to the first area.

An informally shaped pond is surrounded by yellow flag irises and the giant leaves of petasites, and the surface is covered with the small deep yellow "false waterlily" *Nuphar lutea*. Beyond the pond is an orchard garden with island beds full of aquilegias and sweet rocket in soft colours. The garden extends into a meadow here with older fruit trees and pollarded willows.

A large mount reminds you that Slot de Nisse is an old property. Fine chestnut, ash, and lime trees grow on it and the buttercup-studded grass is left uncut, except for a mown path that winds round to the top. Behind the mount is a woodland border, edged with ivy, where swathes of *Polygonum bistorta* 'Superba' are a feature. From the mount you can return towards the house to another series of more formal enclosures.

A "Quince Walk" has yew borders with an underplanting of ferns, pulmonaria, hostas, columbines, euphorbias, and *Meconopsis cambrica*, the yellow Welsh poppy that self-seeds but always seems to choose a perfect position. Another compartment contains a circle of clipped box balls that resembles a splendid green Gâteau St Honoré.

Fine planting around the edge of the informal pond.

☞ open: Easter to 1 Nov, daily, 11am–5pm

Further information from:
Maashoek 2b, Steyl, gem Tegelen
Tel: (077) 373 3020
postal address: Spoorstraat 42,
Nl 5931 PV Tegelen

Nearby sights of interest:
Pottery Museum.

One of the many varied corners.

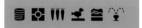

20 *Tegelen: Botanische Tuin Jochum-Hof*

Location: E from Eindhoven close to the German border; from N271 Nijmegen–Roermond road, follow signs to Tegelen and drive into town, then follow signs to Steyl and Baarlo ferry

This botanic garden was founded and laid out by Pater Peter Jochum in 1933. Immediately by the entrance is the first piece of garden that Father Jochum constructed. There is an unusual spreading ginkgo and a large *Koelreuteria paniculata* or Pagoda tree with some deep blue *Baptisia australis* nearby. Beyond this is the Mediterranean garden, then a hosta border overshadowed by an enormous *Acer platanoides* 'Faassey's black'. A greenhouse contains cactus and bougainvillea. *Torreya californica* is underplanted with foxgloves and geraniums, and near to it is a spectacular variegated *Cornus mas*.

The pretty *heemtuin* is laid out beneath mature silver birches, overlooking the broad River Maas. An open area of meadow with poppies, a pond surrounded by giant hogweed, rosebay willow herb, and bramble and another pond with waterlilies, knapweed, tansy, and mullein are all representative of parts of the north Limburg landscape. A herb garden and Paterspark are in a separate section. Paterspark has several mature trees, including a *Liriodendron tulipfera*, *Aesculus indica*, limes, and conifers.

☞ open: First weekend in Jul; also by appointment

Further information from:
Golsteinseweg 24,
4351 SC Veere, Zeeland
Tel: (0118) 614 520

Nearby sights of interest:
Veere: Schotse Huizen and Stadhuis; Delta Expo.

21 *De Tintelhof*

Location: Between Veere and Middelburg; from main road Veere–Middelburg, at 2.5km sign turn W and Tintelhof is first house

In 1975 there was a barren waste, without a single tree. Four years later, this garden was open to the public. For that, the gardener has to be both dedicated and knowledgeable.

When she was young, Ank Dekker worked in the office of the famous Dutch designer Mien Ruys and later came to know the Belgian designer Jacques Wirtz. Wirtz, she says, taught her about "clipping", the importance of bold geometric shapes to give form and structure to a garden. Both of these designers had their influence on her subsequent gardening, but the initial impetus came from her grandmother's garden. The garden is a blend of nostalgia and sharp design principles which is what makes it so special. It combines a series of intimate formal compartments with a more open English country garden style of irregular flower-edged lawns and ponds.

The tiny *potager*-herb garden has box-edged beds with standard gooseberries and globe artichokes in the centre of each. A wisteria-covered arch leads to another small compartment with an arbour. The planting is in pinks and purples, with symmetrical purple-leaved plums, roses, purple weigela, and cotinus, underplanted with red plantain, geraniums, and peonies. The richly planted flowering borders are contrasted with simpler areas: a curve of hawthorn around a central specimen tree; a woodland area of quince trees, long grass, and bluebells.

The steps to the lawn from the house terrace are edged by an arrangement of clipped box balls. From the house and the terrace there are two perspectives across the lawn. One is to the large natural pond and the other has an "eye-stopper" more splendid than even the 17th-century landscape designers could have provided: the spires of Middelburg which can be seen across the field through a deliberate gap in the trees.

Bold shapes give structure to the garden.

22 *Arboretum Trompenburg*

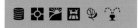

Location: From A16/E19, take exit 25, Rotterdam Centrum, Capelle, and continue towards centre, take the underpass and Honingerdijk is second turning on right

Arboretum Trompenburg is more than just a mecca for dendrologists from all over the world. It is a green oasis in the middle of Rotterdam and a delightfully laid out garden as well.

Sited among the rare and mature trees are a rose garden, a heather garden, a border of cacti and succulents, and herbaceous borders laid out between canals.

There are five main parts of the garden. In the central and earliest part planting began in 1820 and a number of oaks still remain. Different forms of Atlas, Lebanon, and Himalayan cedars grow here. The western part was designed in 1870 by J D Zocher the younger and the ponds and the brook give a rural atmosphere. There are some large trees in this area including a splendid *Taxodium distichum imbricatum*, the bald cypress, ashes, and maples.

The eastern section is laid out ornamentally with a heather garden, rosarium, goldfish pool, and herbaceous borders. Two other areas, Perenhof and Woudesteyn, are much more recent. The first is planted with trees and shrubs while the second contains a large dahlia collection.

Five generations of the Van Hoey Smith family have collected trees and shrubs for the arboretum and although it is now managed by Rotterdam council, the family still lives here. There are 2,500 varieties of trees and shrubs in all, including 165 oaks, 132 chamaecyparis, 90 maples, 87 hollies, and many others.

open: 1 Apr to 30 Sep, Mon to Fri 9am–5pm and weekends closes 4pm; 1 Oct to 31 Mar, as above but closes Sun

Further information from:
Honingerdijk 86,
3062 NX Rotterdam
Tel: (010) 233 0166
Fax: (010) 233 0171

Nearby sights of interest:
Rotterdam: Boymans-van Beuningen Museum, Euromast, Kijk-kubus houses, Schielandshuis (museum).

Key to gardens

1 Kasteel Alden Biesen
2 Kruidtuin, Antwerpen
3 Rubenshuis
4 Albert De Raedt
5 Park Beervelde
6 Hof ter Saksen
7 Arboretum Bokrijk
8 Domein Tudor
   and Domein Beisbroek
9 Mr and Mrs Van De Caesbeek
10 Plantentuin, Gent
11 Japanse Tuin
12 Kasteel Hex
13 Vlaamse Toontuinen
14 Arboretum Kalmthout

15 Kruidtuin, Leuven
16 Piet Bekaert and Dr De Clercq
17 Roos Volckaert
18 Nationale Plantentuin
   van Belgie
19 The English Garden
20 Orshof
21 Patricia van Roosmalen
22 Claire Hertoghe and
   Mr and Mrs Lenaerts
23 Scholteshof

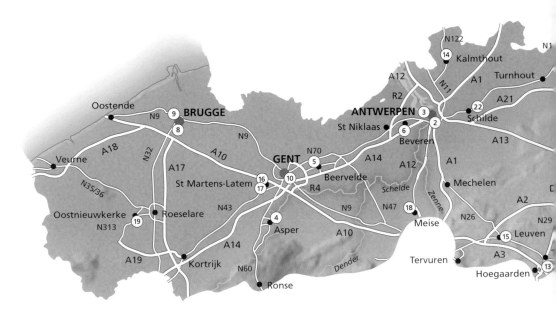

Key

===== Motorways
= Principal trunk highways
③ Gardens
● Major towns and cities
• Towns

Northern Belgium

Flanders is the northern part of Belgium where the inhabitants speak Flemish, a dialect of Dutch. There is much more to Flanders than its famous towns of Bruges, Ghent, and Antwerp with their canals and historic buildings. The region stretches from the short strip of North Sea coast – a mere 67km (42 miles) long – with a string of popular seaside resorts to the border with Dutch Limburg, a few kilometres from Germany. Much of northern Flanders is wood and heathland. The fine arboretum at Kalmthout (see pp.108–11) is set in typical heath landscape not far from the Dutch border.

In the 16th century Antwerp was the richest and largest port in the world, but in the 17th century it fell on hard times. It is now, however, one of the liveliest and most flourishing cities in Europe. It is a treasure house of historic and artistic relics and Rubenshuis (see p.99), with its beautifully restored garden, is an essential port of call. East of Antwerp is Schilde where there are several private gardens to visit (see pp.118–9), as well as Kasteel van 's-Gravenwezel which is open for the last weekend in May and the first weekend in July.

Verbena bonariensis, salvias, and marigolds in the botanic garden at Leuven.

The dramatic waterfall in the Japanese garden at Hasselt.

The beautiful towns of Ghent and Bruges were rivals for many years in the Middle Ages and after. In the 19th century Ghent became a centre for horticulture. The Park Beervelde (see pp.100–1), where there is a collection of Ghent azaleas, is the elegant venue for flower shows twice a year and at the five-yearly Ghent Floralies Belgian nurserymen show their finest plants and flowers.

The next is in the year 2000. Around St Martens-Latem the country is pleasantly wooded. The area was popular with artists at the end of the 19th century and again in the 1920s. Kasteel Ooidonk (see p.113) is set in mature parkland and is an additional attraction.

The Flanders Open Gardens Scheme has expanded dramatically in only a few years. In Bruges, Ghent, and Antwerp there are gardens designed by distinctive Belgian designers such as André Van Wassenhove, René Pechère,

The Lenaerts' pretty rose garden near Antwerp is structured with box, yew, and hornbeam.

One of Dr De Clercq's collection of acers in his garden at Nevele, near Ghent, harmonizes superbly with some of his many rhododendrons.

and Jacques Wirtz that are open to the general public only for the special weekend or to members of the Belgian Open Gardens Scheme (for more information contact Jardins Ouvert Open Tuinen, Chausée de Vleurgat 108, 1000 Bruxelles; tel and fax (02) 646 9736).

The fertile plains of Flemish Brabant and the rich land of Limburg in the east are less well known but have historic towns such as Leuven and Hasselt, with its Japanse Tuin (see p.105) and nearby Arboretum Bokrijk (see pp.102–3). There are some of the finest gardens in Belgium in the east, from the Kruidtuin in Leuven (see p.112) to the magnificent garden of Kasteel Hex (see pp.106–7), which is situated between St Truiden, known for its cherry orchards, and Tongeren. The north-east corner of Limburg is more sparsely populated heathland, but there is the modern garden of Orshof (see pp.116–7) which is well worth a visit.

Kasteel Alden Biesen

Location: W of Maastricht and SE of Hasselt; from the E313 Antwerp–Liège/Luik road, take exit 31, Maastricht/Bilzen, and then direction Bilzen; follow signs to Alden Biesen

open: English garden: 1 Apr to 31 Oct, Tue to Sun, 10am–7pm (closes 9pm, 16 May to 16 Aug); 1 Nov to 31 Mar, Sun and Public Holidays, 10am–6pm; French gardens: all year, Tue to Sun, 10am–6pm

Further information from:
Kasteelstraat 6,
3740 Bilzen-Rijkhoven
Tel: (089) 519 393

Once a centre for the Knights of the Teutonic Order, the castle is now a venue for conferences maintained by the Flemish Community. The original medieval buildings were replaced by a moated castle and then in the 18th century rebuilt again in late Baroque style. The Teutonic Order was dispossessed during the French Revolution and the property sold at auction in 1797. It was in private hands and becoming steadily more neglected until the Belgian State acquired it in 1971. Today the impressive castle and its outbuildings are most beautifully maintained.

Box encloses lavender and junipers.

The formal parterres at the front of the castle have box-edged beds of sage and lavender with standard junipers in the middle. Between the orangery and the chapel is a *parterre de broderie* surrounded by triple *plates-bandes* of neatly clipped box, old roses, herbaceous plants, and box topiary.

The English landscape garden – a small sweep of grass and protecting woodland of beech, lime, and chestnut – contains a pretty rotunda. This Temple to Minerva is sadly fenced off.

Antwerpen: Kruidtuin

Location: In the centre of Antwerp, W of railway station, S of Rubenshuis (see opposite); well signposted; continue down Wapper, turn right, Schuttershofstraat, then left, Komedieplein, which leads into Leopoldstraat

open: All year, daily, 8am–5.45pm; glasshouses: Sat 2–4.45pm and Sun 10am–1pm

Further information from:
Leopoldstraat 24, 2000 Antwerpen
Tel: (03) 232 4087
Fax: (03) 829 0714

Nearby sights of interest:
Stadspark; Dierentuin (Zoo); Domein Middelheim.

This long-established small botanic garden is full of interest. The garden was started in 1825 and opened to the public eight years later. The plants are well labelled and arranged in families. There are beds of bulbous plants, grasses, and representatives of the composites, umbellifers, and amaranthaceae families. Parts are shaded by large trees and there is an interesting grotto with a cascade and a small pond planted with pontederia and waterlilies, with gunnera and *Lobelia cardinalis* growing on the margins.

Antwerpen: Rubenshuis

Location: W of Central Station, near shopping centre; well signposted

The contrast of the elaborate Italian Baroque style that Pieter-Paul Rubens chose for his house and garden with the unadorned façades and jazzy chaotic windows of nearby shops is dramatic. There is a giddying transition straight into the 17th century, to surroundings richly ornate yet firmly ordered.

Rubens bought the land in 1610 and was living in his house by 1615. After his death the house was acquired by William Cavendish, Duke of Newcastle. Then followed a long period of obscurity until the house was acquired by the City of Antwerp in 1937. The city architect, Emile van Averbeeke, began to plan the restoration using engravings by Jacob Harrewijn, which were made between 1684 and 1692.

To reach the garden you pass through the building and into a high-walled courtyard bounded by an arcaded Baroque portico. From there you step onto a balustraded terrace and the garden is laid out before you. This has been faithfully reconstructed from the one depicted in Rubens' and his collaborators' painting, *The Walk in the Garden*, which is in the Alte Pinakothek in Munich.

There is a straight axis between the four parterres to the Pavilion of Hercules, a small temple with a balustraded roof and a pillared front. Each parterre is surrounded by a low yew hedge and is entered via a small gate beneath an arbour. The parterres are variations of rectangular shapes punctuated with narrow cones of yew. They are planted with colourful plants, such as cleomes, foxgloves, *Lychnis coronaria*, and marigolds. Oleanders, pomegranates, bay, lemons, and figs in pots line the paths. On the right is the pergola. Caryatids in the form of herms, and painted satiny black like the gates and arbours, support the pillars which are clad in vines, honeysuckle, and other climbing plants.

open: All year, daily except Mon, 10am–4.45pm; closes 1 and 2 Jan, 1 May and Ascension Day, 1 and 2 Nov, and 25 and 26 Dec

Further information from:
9–11 Wapper, 2000 Antwerpen
Tel: (03) 232 4747
Fax: (03) 227 3692

Nearby sights of interest:
Kathedraal; Plantin-Moretus Museum; Koninklijk Museum voor Schone Kunsten; Diamond Museum; Museum Mayer van den Bergh.

Black-painted caryatids support the vine-clad pergola.

Asper: Albert De Raedt

Location: 16km (10 miles) S of Ghent on N60 to Oudenaarde; 2.5km (1½ miles) after turning for Eke, in district of Asper, there is a large curtain shop on the right; after railway bridge filter to the left and return along the road on the other side; number 76 is within a few meters

open: One weekend in May (telephone to find out exact date), guided tours at 10am, 2 and 4pm, or by appointment

Further information from:
Gentsebaan 76, 9890 Asper (Gavere)
Tel: (09) 384 3557

A corner of this exciting collection of trees and shrubs.

Albert De Raedt is a dedicated plantsman and his 1.5ha (3¾ acre) garden is full of uncommon trees and shrubs. Visitors need to be equally dedicated to get the most from a guided tour. The De Raedts have lived in the house for 17 years and the garden was made completely from scratch. Unlike many gardens in Belgium, it is not flat but full of surprising contours.

The effect today is interestingly unruly, like a temperate jungle. Small sandy paths wander here and there round the garden, with a treasure round every corner. *Magnolia* 'Leonard Messel' grows near a *Tilia platyphyllos*, the large-leaved lime. *Sorbus sorbaria* mingles with *Lamium galeobdolen* and symphoricarpus. A *Quercus cerris* surveys the plants below. Wild strawberries grow beneath a perovskia. Further along, there is an arching *Physocarpus opulifolius*, a *Sophora japonica*, and a weeping beech.

By the next stretch of path there is an ailanthus, large clumps of bamboo, *Calycantha fertilis* with chocolate-purple flowers, *Hydrangea quercifolia*, *Magnolia denudata*, and the bitter orange *Poncirus trifoliata*. The path widens out into another clearing where pink rugosa roses and *Rubus odoratus* clash happily with yellow fern fronds. Nearby are surprisingly large specimens of *Acer pennsylvaticum*, *Fagus asplenifolia*, and *Nothofagus obliqua*. There is a recherché collection of oaks along one border and unusual hornbeams can be found in the garden too.

Park Beervelde

Location: 10km (6¼ miles) NE of Ghent by A14/E17 to Antwerp, then take exit 11, Beervelde/Lochristie, direction Beervelde; after about 1.5km (1 mile), at traffic lights in Beervelde, turn left; park entrance 180m (200yds) on right

open: Plant Fairs: 7, 8, 9 May, 10am–6pm; 8, 9, 10 Oct, 10am–5pm; also by appointment (tel: (09) 356 8182); refreshments served Sat and Sun

Further information from:
Beerveldedorp 75, 9080 Beervelde (Lochristi)
Tel: (09) 355 5540
Fax: (09) 355 0831

Nearby sights of interest:
Ghent; Kasteel Laarne.

A fine avenue leads to a wooded landscape park in the English style. Azaleas and rhododendrons, sheets of lily of the valley, and newly uncoiling ferns make it ravishing in May when it is open for the Plant Fair, for which Beervelde is famous. Sweeps of lawn are bounded by a winding river, crossed by picturesque bridges.

The walled kitchen garden is filled with flowers, fruit, and vegetables. There is a small formal parterre near the coach house. Buildings remain from the late 19th century when the estate was designed by Louis Fuchs.

At the far end of the park, at the edge of the winding lake with its island, is a 19th-century pavilion and a large pergola planted with wisteria. In the woodland and near the lake are many fine trees, including *Acer opalus*, an old *Catalpa bignonoides*, *Hamamelis* ssp., an Italian maple, *Pinus cembra*, and several witch hazels.

A collection of Hardy Ghent azaleas is expanding. Twelve years ago hardly anyone in Belgium knew about the Hardy Ghent Azalea, although they were first hybridized in Ghent in 1825. They are still very popular and well known under that name in the UK. As well as the Comte de Kerchove, Albert De Raedt, whose garden at Asper is described opposite, is involved in tracing the lost azaleas.

Beveren: Hof ter Saksen

Location: W of Antwerp on the road to St Niklaas; leave Beveren on N70, direction St Niklaas, after passing Beveren church, turn left at third traffic lights; follow directions to Haasdonk; the arboretum is left after railway

open: 1 Apr to 31 Oct, daily, 10am–6pm; 1 Nov to 31 Mar, weekdays, Sun, and Public Holidays, 10am–4.30pm; refreshments served Sun and Public Holidays in the summer

Further information from: Haasdonkbaan 101, 9120 Beveren Tel: (03) 775 2851

The attractive orangery seen from across the castle moat.

Hof ter Saksen is one of Belgium's best-kept secrets. A romantic, ruined, moated château looks down upon an exciting plant collector's garden. The collections, mainly trees and shrubs, are relatively young but the estate itself is older and forms a perfect setting for them.

In the 1950s and 60s, nearby St Niklaas was a town made prosperous by the textile industry. Hof ter Saksen was the country retreat of one of the rich textile families, the Meerts. In 1979 the Meert family sold the estate to the community of Beveren.

The arboretum has 4,000 specimens, with a particularly important collection of Chinese plants. Sometimes the trees and shrubs, such as rhododendrons and cornus, are planted in groups in borders, and sometimes as solitary specimens in the grass like *Halesia diptera*, one of the snowdrop trees from America. By the bridge to the castle are herbaceous borders. In the courtyard of the farm there is a bee garden and in the summer sculpture exhibitions are held in the gardens.

As well as the 12ha (30 acres) of the garden, there are 8ha (20 acres) beyond the perimeter and an educational area of 2ha (5 acres). This fascinating section is Waasland in miniature with polders, streams, agricultural fields, limestone hills, dyke banks, and black ground.

⁊ *Arboretum Bokrijk*

open: 26 Mar to 30 Sep, daily, 10am–6pm; entry to the arboretum is free but there is an admission charge to the Open Air Museum

Further information from:
3600 Bokrijk (Genk)
Tel: (011) 224 575
Fax: (011) 241 746

Nearby sights of interest:
Open Air Museum (see opposite).

The arboretum is particularly known for its collection of spectacular conifers.

Location: NE of Hasselt in the direction of Genk; take N75 to Genk; Park Midden Limburg/Bokrijk is signed left; park in the correct area, signed Kasteel (not Museum) because they are some distance apart

The domain of Bokrijk belonged to the Abbey of Herkenrode until 1791. The castle itself was built in 1896 in what has been described as the "Meuse Renaissance" style. It was acquired by the province in 1938 and the planting of the arboretum began in 1950. The arboretum is at some distance from the main tourist sites and the magnificent collection can be studied in tranquillity.

The trees are partly planted in systematic order beds and partly as if in a landscape park. The individual trees are not all labelled but the family groups are indicated. Herbaceous plants, flowering shrubs, and climbers are often to be found in the beds and under the trees creating many attractive pictures. One entrancing specimen, startlingly unfamiliar from a distance, turned out to be a 24m (80ft) birch completely festooned by a wisteria.

Bokrijk is known for its collections of ilex, malus, and bamboo, but in particular for its conifers. The wonderful variety of texture, size, form, and colour can be truly appreciated and differentiated. Long-needled pines such as the Japanese Red Pine (*Pinus*

densiflora), *P. jeffreyi* from California, and the smaller *P. mugo* contrast with tall blue cedars. Another revelation is the variety of chamaecyparis. There is a good collection of different, mature false cypresses. Here, too, is the place to come to enjoy fully the majesty of a mature 'Leylandii' (X *Cupressocyparis leylandii*) which has been allowed to grow to its natural shape and size.

Another well-represented group are the acers. There are many splendid mature acers including *Acer cissifolium*, *A. japonica* 'Aurea', the appropriately named *A. platanoides* 'Globosum' which is a wonderful shape, the pale and ethereal *A. platanaoides* 'Widederseei', and *A. monspessulanum* with small, ivy-like leaves.

The collection of hibiscus, species and cultivars, like *Hibiscus syriacus* 'Pink Giant', *H. s.* 'Russian Violet', and *H. coelestis* also includes shrubs with white and palest pink flowers. These are grown in among the different hollies which include a beautiful *Ilex aquifolia* 'Argentea pendula'. There are also groups of species roses, hydrangeas, an array of different philadelphus, and even grasses that range from tiny blue *Festuca glauca* to tall *Arundo donax*. One can also find berberis and honeysuckles growing here.

Next to the castle, in the old vegetable garden, there is a rose garden containing more than 100 different roses. The other section of the Bokrijk estate is the Open Air Museum where a number of old villages and houses have been reconstructed. In the new herb garden the beds are edged with thyme and box, and planted with different basils and hyssop.

---

8 *Brugge: Domein Tudor and Domein Beisbroek*

Location: On the southern edge of Bruges; from the N32 Bruges to Torhout, take a right turn about 1km (¾ mile) (Tudor) or 2km (1¼ miles) (Beisbroek) before road crosses A10/E40 motorway

open: Park: at all times; herb garden: May to Oct

Further information from:
Zeeweg 96 and 147,
8200 St Andries, Brugge

Nearby sights of interest:
Historic centre of Bruges.

Well-labelled herb beds.

These adjoining estates were once the property of the Abbey of St Andries but were destroyed after the French Revolution. The Domein Tudor is the most interesting area for the garden visitor.

The crenellated building was erected in 1904 and it over-looks a lawn with a simple box parterre in the centre. The grass is surrounded by fine mature beeches and blue cedars.

The Kruidentuin (herb garden) is signed from the Domein Tudor. Its walls are clothed with trained peach, pear, and plum trees. Yew-hedged enclosures and rectangular beds edged neatly with brick create a workmanlike appearance. Clearly labelled herbs are planted in families in one area, while in the other plants are grouped according to their uses.

There are pleasant walks along fine avenues of trees and in the extensive woods of the adjoining Domein Beisbroek.

open: By appointment from end May to end Jul

Further information from:
Grote Ede 18, 8200 St Andries, Brugge
Tel: (050) 391 906

Nearby sights of interest:
Historic centre of Bruges; garden of designer André Van Wassenhove (by written appointment; Kleine Kerkhofstraat 72, 8310 Assebroek).

9 *Brugge: Mr and Mrs Van De Caesbeek*

Location: In the western suburb of Bruges; from S of town centre take N31 direction Zeebrugge, then take a left turn in direction of St Andries Stade Olympia; cross N32 Torhoutsesteenweg and then turn left at next set of traffic lights to Hermitage; take third road on right and then right again

Tall hornbeam hedges enclose the long low house designed by Mr Van De Caesbeek and the surrounding garden, keeping the outside world firmly at bay. In front square, box-edged beds are each planted with the almost white standard rose, *Rosa* 'Maria Matilda', and a mélange of white daisies, sharp yellow Welsh poppies, and campanulas.

The house turns its face to the terrace and the garden behind. On the terrace, *R.* 'New Dawn' harmonizes with the terracotta roof tiles and bricks underfoot, and white hydrangeas in *caisses de Versailles* echo the white French café chairs and the house walls, and contrast with the sober paving setts and slate slabs that are mixed with the brick.

There is a long central grass walk bordered by old apple trees and topiary yew columns. Interesting foliage abounds: the large leaves of *Gunnera manicata* and *Petasites fragrans* contrast with the dense textured clipped box and yew; pollarded willows support the golden leaves of the hop, *Humulus lupulus* 'Aureus'.

The recently constructed pergola planted with pale roses.

To one side is the newest piece of the garden design: narrow flowerbeds, cut through the grass like the rays of the sun. The layout, the work of Mr Van De Caesbeek, has been brilliantly planted by his wife with a glorious spume of *Alchemilla mollis*, white erigerons, white foxgloves, pale yellow lupins, and *Salvia sclarea*. Behind is an iron-framed pergola planted with softly coloured roses, and, remarkably, the beginnings of a yew hedge growing straight down the centre of it.

This unexpected and secret place is designed as a garden of "lost content". It has a magical quality that evokes childhood dreams, as its owners intend.

Gent: Plantentuin

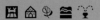

Location: Just S of the city centre, by Citadel Park/Congress Centre; from E40 Bruges–Brussels motorway take exit 14, Ghent/St Denis, direction town centre; Citadel Park is beyond railway bridge and garden is on the right

The university botanic garden has been at this site since 1900. It is attractively landscaped with many fine mature trees, including a large weeping beech, a swamp cypress (*Taxodium distichum*), and handsome cedars. A stone pine, *Pinus pinea*, usually only seen in Mediterranean regions, flourishes here out of doors. The first feature by the entrance is a rock bank with the plants well labelled. There is a lake nearby and a sunny border planted with campanulas, cistus, and lavender.

Separate sections of herbs, trials of bedding plants, and systematic beds containing decorative plant families make the garden well worth a visit. There is a pool with marsh plants, collections of monocotyledons, which include grasses and bulbs, tiny raised beds planted with crassulas, and an arboretum. In the summer geraniums and succulents are placed outside the glasshouses. Inside there are bamboos, palms, ferns, and gigantic rubber trees. There is a large pool with the giant waterlily, *Victoria amazonica*, and *Euryale ferox*, an annual plant with round leaves covered with spines. In addition, there are houses for cacti and Mediterranean plants.

open: All year, Mon to Fri 9am–5pm, and Sat, Sun, and Public Holidays 9am to 12 noon; cacti house: Sun and Public Holidays 11am to 12 noon

Further information from:
K L Ledeganckstraat 35, 9000 Gent
Tel and fax: (09) 264 5073

Nearby sights of interest:
Citadel Park and all attractions of Ghent; Kasteel Leeuwergem, tel: (09) 360 2216 by appointment only (see p.113).

Succulents in containers.

 # Hasselt: Japanse Tuin

Location: 75km (46½ miles) E of Brussels, just inside outer ring road; coming into Hasselt, turn on to outer ring towards Eindhoven; do not turn off but continue on ring road and take next major turning right, N702, into town centre

This authentic Japanese garden has been built as a symbol of friendship between the cities of Itami in Japan and Hasselt.

One area of the garden is designed as a miniature Japanese mountain landscape with a view to a waterfall based on one from a temple in Kyoto. The water flows between enormous granite rocks. Japanese apricots (*Prunus mume*) are planted round the edge, together with acers, azaleas, and delicate silver birches.

A 17th-century-style tea-house and the ceremony house are reflected in a calm lake with a pebble beach. From this beach a bridge and then some stepping stones across the lake lead to the central garden. Here on this small hill is the ceremony house, with its enclosed inner area cut off by sliding paper walls.

open: 1 Apr to 30 Oct, Tue to Fri 10am–5pm and Sat and Sun 2–6pm

Further information from:
Gouverneur Verwilghensingel, 3500 Hasselt
Tel: (011) 239 543
Fax: (011) 225 023

Nearby sights of interest:
Arboretum Bokrijk and Open Air Museum (see pp.102–3).

 ## Kasteel Hex

🌱 open: Rose Festival: 11, 12, 13 Jun, 10am–6pm; Fruit and Vegetable Festival: 18, 19 Sep, 10am–6pm

Further information from:
B 3870 Heers
Tel: (012) 747 341
Fax: (012) 744 987

Location: 85km (53 miles) E of Brussels and 25km (15½ miles) NE of Liège; from E313 Antwerp to Liège/Luik take exit 29 to Hasselt Oost and Tongeren/Tongres and then direction Tongeren; once at Kortessen follow directions to Borgloon/Looz, then follow signs to Heers where the castle is signed; from the E40/A3 Brussels to Liège/Luik road take exit 29, Waremme/Borgworm, and take the direction Tongeren on N69, Hex is signed after about 10km (6¼ miles)

The beautiful gardens around Kasteel Hex are among the most famous in Belgium but alas, they are not open very frequently. The castle was the summer residence of a Prince-Bishop of Liège who laid out formal gardens, the Chinese gardens, and brought in cows and sheep to create an English parkland in 1770. The high reputation the garden has today, however, is due to the Comtesse d'Ursel who came to the château in 1959. The Comtesse planted more than 200 varieties of old and species roses and asked the landscape designer, Jacques Wirtz, to simplify the three terraces which overlook the parkland.

The old rose garden is protected by a 4.5m (15ft) tall hedge of trimmed *Cornus mas*. Roses date from the 18th century when the East India Company brought three China roses back from

The formal flower garden outside the apartments of the Prince-Bishop.

the east for the Prince-Bishop: *Rosa chinensis* 'Old Blush'
(syn. *R.* x *odorata* 'Pallida'), *R. chinensis multipetala*, and another
unnamed one. There is a collection of old roses.

The formal French garden is ornamented with flattened
domes of clipped box, flowerbeds, and urns on pedestals, and
the axis continues towards a pair of delightful gate lodges and
through the gates along a lane.

On the opposite side of the main axis from the rose garden is
the Chinese garden enclosed by undulating yew hedges. Inside
a painted wooden Buddha sits cross-legged beneath a small
pavilion. *Alchemilla mollis* froths from the crazy paving.

The famous *potager* can be seen from a long balustraded
walk. The necessary retaining wall has formed the perfect spot
for fruit trees, particularly for espaliered pears, for 200 years. As
well as vegetables all looking decorative in their own right, there
is a collection of fine modern roses, and rows of dahlias and
sweet peas. The landscape park at Hex was one of the first to
be created in Belgium and has hardly been altered since.

---

13 *Hoegaarden: Vlaamse Toontuinen*

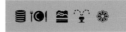

Location: 5km (3 miles) S of Tienen/Tirlemont by N29, 40km (25 miles) E of
Brussels by A3/E40

open: All year, daily,
10am–9pm

Further information from:
Houtmarkt 1, 3320 Hoegaarden
Tel: (016) 767 843
Fax: (016) 767 919

Nearby sights of interest:
Hoegaarden brewery.

The site of the Flemish show gardens, with some fine mature
limes, copper beeches, and sweet chestnuts and overlooked by
the monumental Rococo church is very attractive. The themed
gardens such as a rose garden, water garden, herb garden, and
a patio garden are scattered around the site. There is a modern
garden in memory of King Baudouin, a golden garden, a bamboo
garden, and an allergen-free garden among the varied collection.

**Contrasting forms of *Hosta
sieboldii* and *Lysimachia punctata*.**

The King Baudouin garden is
designed around a symbolic spiral
and planted with rhododendrons
and hydrangeas. A *Cryptomeria
japonica* raised in the greenhouses
of Laeken (see pp.132–3) by King
Baudouin himself from seeds
given to him by Emperor Hirohito
of Japan is a feature of this garden.
An interesting section in one
corner shows different methods
of composting.

Naming of plants is sporadic,
and then only in Flemish without
proper Latin names.

Arboretum Kalmthout

open: 15 Mar to 15 Nov, daily, 10am–5pm; special open days in Jan/Feb to see the witch hazels

Further information from:
Heuvel 2, B2920 Kalmthout
Tel: (03) 666 6741
Fax: (03) 666 3396

Location: 20km (12½ miles) N of Antwerp; from E19 Antwerp–Breda take exit 4, then N117 to Kalmthout

Charles van Geert, a nurseryman from Antwerp, bought 1.5ha (3¾ acres) of acid heathland at Kalmthout in 1856. He wanted to show how some of the plants he was hoping to introduce into Belgium would adapt to the difficult climate there. He died in 1896 and the nursery was acquired by Antoine Kort who extended it to 35ha (87 acres). With World War I, the nursery closed down and it then remained derelict for over 30 years.

Many of the magnificent mature trees date from the time of van Geert, particularly the trees in the Old Conifer Avenue, while Kort planted the first witch hazels. Kalmthout, however, has only developed as a world-class arboretum since Georges and Robert de Belder bought the site in 1952. Soon they were joined by Robert's wife, Jelena de Belder Kovacic, who came from former Yugoslavia where she had studied agriculture at the University of Zagreb. With enthusiasm, horticultural knowledge, and

Groups of trees are surrounded by low-growing colourful shrubs, such as fuchsias.

Informal planting around the pond margins.

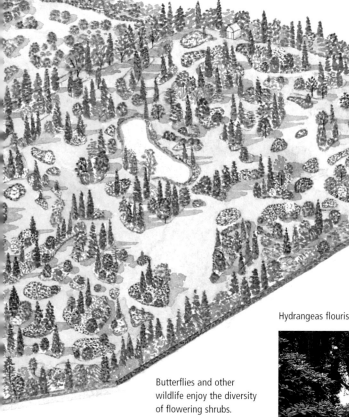

Hydrangeas flourish beneath the trees.

Butterflies and other wildlife enjoy the diversity of flowering shrubs.

In winter the shapes of the trees can be fully appreciated.

Jelena de Belder's gift for associating plants, the arboretum has evolved over the years. The result is a series of informal island beds, remarkable for their subtle groupings of trees, shrubs, and perennial plants, and beckoning grass walks. The individual beds, usually designed around one of the huge original trees, are snugly encircled with rounded banks of *Stephanandra incisa*, berberis, bold hostas, elegantly arching fuchsias, and girdles of ivy: contrasts of colour, texture, and form.

In spring, the wonderful collection of flowering cherries and many different magnolias bloom, to be followed swiftly by rhododendrons and azaleas. High summer sees the roses and herbaceous plants at their best. In late summer there are beds of hardy fuchsias and in the white garden, the luscious overblown panicles of *Hydrangea paniculata* 'Grandiflora' are complemented by drifts of white agapanthus and the blue-grey leaves and creamy flowers of *Macleaya cordata*, the plume poppy.

In autumn the garden is a rich mixture of conifers, berrying shrubs, and the changing leaf colour of deciduous trees. Different forms of the Japanese maple, *Acer palmatum* cultivars, turn brilliant orange, red, and yellow. The fine malus collection, the flowering crabs, are loaded with small, vivid fruits. The leaves of the deciduous Ghent and Japanese azaleas add their warm autumnal notes, as do the leaves of the important witch hazel collection. The bright pink berries of the European euonymous and the glossy blackish-purple ones of the American pokeweed, *Phytolacca americana*, glow. The flowerheads of the hydrangeas that are such a feature in August acquire a greenish or deep red metallic sheen. The bracken turns golden and the oaks scarlet and rust. Colchicums appear in sharp white and softer mauves.

As winter approaches, heathers, blue cedar, and the polished mahogany of the trunks of the acers, the white silver birches, the patterns of the bare branches of the deciduous trees, and the towering conifers make the garden equally attractive. Almost as soon as winter has the garden in its grip, there are special open days to see the witch hazels in flower. The aboretum is world famous for its Hamamelis collection. *Hamamelis* x *intermedia* 'Ruby Glow' dates from the days of Kort, while the de Belders introduced *H.* x *intermedia* 'Jelena' and *H.* 'Diana'.

There are two ponds, a pretty pavilion draped with variegated ivy, and a pleasant country house with a terrace, surrounded by old rhododendron hybrids and reached by the avenue of large conifers, planted in the days of the original nursery. Some of the island beds are colour-themed like the white garden; there is a yellow garden and a blue garden, as well as groups of hostas, roses, and astilbes. The arboretum today covers an area of 12ha (30 acres) but seems much larger because of the design. To come upon the same bed from another side, is to be presented with yet another picture. Fellow visitors are absorbed into its quiet intimacy and the atmosphere is one of beauty and tranquillity.

Since 1986 the arboretum has been owned by the province of Antwerp and managed by a group of Friends of the Arboretum of Kalmthout, and its future is now secure.

New leaves in early spring are as colourful as blossom.

Fresh white and green make the arboretum enchanting in spring.

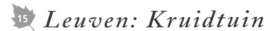

15 *Leuven: Kruidtuin*

Location: 25km (15½ miles) E of Brussels by N2 or A2/E40

open: 1 May to 30 Sep, daily, 8am–8pm (Sun and Public Holidays opens 9am); 1 Oct to 30 Apr, 8am–5pm; orangery and tropical greenhouse: Sun and Public Holidays

Further information from:
Kapucijnenvoer 30, 3000 Leuven
Tel: (016) 232 400
Fax: (016) 221 104

Nearby sights of interest:
St Pieterskerk; Stadhuis.

Colourful bedding plants seen through a grand gateway are an irresistible invitation into this immaculately maintained botanic garden. The plants are well grown and the colour schemes very attractive, a lesson in how to use bright colours in flowerbeds. The original botanic garden in Leuven was the first to be founded in Belgium, in 1738. The present garden with its severely elegant orangery dates from 1821. There are order beds, a rock garden, a semicircular pond, a water garden, a collection of herbs, and some good mature trees, including *Gymnocladus dioicus*, *Ulmus glabra* 'Exoniensis', and a *Pterocarya fraxinifolia*, as well as planes and liriodendrons. The plants are labelled.

Do not miss the fruit garden, where there are trained fruit trees including two-year-olds trained in the traditional "verrier palmette" shape, or the tiny enclosed corner next to it, where there is an exuberant garden of summer flowers with drifts of giant sunflowers, *Verbena bonariensis*, canna lilies, and salvias. There is a pergola here too, planted excitingly with climbing annuals: the cream and coral flowered *Mina lobata*, black-eyed Susans, *Asarina scandans*, and *Ipomea quamoclit*. *Verbena* 'Peaches & Cream' blends subtly with *Salvia coccinea* 'Coral Nymph', *Alonsoa meridionalis*, and pink diascias in an eiderdown of brilliant colour.

All round the garden are many well-grown tender plants, put out in pots for the summer. In the winter they are kept in the orangery. A new woodland garden is planned.

The immaculate garden is the setting for sculpture exhibitions in the summer.

16 *St Martens-Latem: Piet Bekaert and Dr De Clercq*

Location: About 8km (5 miles) SW of Ghent; leave Ghent in the direction of Ostend and after about 10km (6¼ miles) take exit 13 to Ghent West/Deinze: left; continue for 6km (3¾ miles) on N466 until first roundabout and church; take left turning to Deurle, after 100m (110yds) cross green-painted iron bridge and after 300m (330yds) take first left and continue for 350m (380yds)

A boundary line of mopheaded maples growing out of undulating mounds of ivy and a box hedge which is clipped into comfortable curves so that it looks like a giant caterpillar flowing round the garden: immediately you know that you are looking at the work of a master designer. A group of blue conifers, clipped flat like oval lollipops in front of a crisp yew hedge, distract from but do not hide an arable field beyond. Clipped columns of yew, domed, pointed, slim, or buxom, contrast with horizontal yew blocks.

In front of the house, white hydrangeas, roses, clematis, and philadelphus are cool and delicate against the preponderance of evergreens. Piet Bekaert is an architect, garden designer, painter, photographer, sculptor, novelist, and poet. His garden can be described in similar terms – poetical, architectural, and painterly.

May is the best time to see Dr De Clercq's garden when the rhododendrons and azaleas are in bloom. He is a true plantsman, a collector, and a plant breeder with 1,500 different rhododendrons in his 1.5ha (3¾ acre) garden. Many of the rhododendrons are unique as they are the results of his own crosses. In addition there are collections of the snake bark maples, hollies, and hamamelis.

open: Piet Bekaert: by appointment, preferably in writing; admission charge; Dr De Clercq: telephone after 10pm to make an appointment

Further information from:
Piet Bekaert's garden:
Voordelaan 13, 9831 Deurle
(St Martens-Latem)
Tel: (09) 282 6182
Fax: (09) 281 0365
Dr De Clercq's garden: Graaf van Hoornestraat 15, 9850 Nevele
Tel: (09) 371 5535

Nearby sights of interest:
Ghent: Cathedral of St Bavo, the Belfry, the Town Hall, Graslei – a row of 12th-century Guildhouses; Kasteel Leeuwergem (9620 Zottegem; tel: (09) 360 2216, fax: (09) 361 0138, by appointment only) in the SSE of Ghent, a moated château in the French style with unique *théâtre de verdure*; Kasteel Ooidonk (Ooidonkdreef 9, 9800 Deinze; tel: (09) 282 3570, fax: (09) 282 5282; open summer 9am–7pm and winter 9am–4pm and from Easter to 15 Sep, Sun and Public Holidays 2–5.30pm), an imposing moated château.

Beautifully composed groups of evergreens are an outstanding feature in Piet Bekaert's garden.

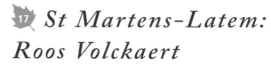

17

St Martens-Latem: Roos Volckaert

open: Last weekend Jun, second weekend Jul, 10am–6pm; also by appointment from May to Aug

Further information from:
Der Groene Tuinkamer, Kleine Heide 23, 9830 St Martens-Latem
Tel and fax: (09) 282 4810

A wooden seat beneath a rose-covered arch overlooks the pond.

Location: About 8km (5 miles) SW of Ghent; from the A10/E40 Ostend–Brussels motorway take exit 14, Flanders Expo, and then direction Dienze; after 3.5km (2¼ miles), at St Martens-Latem, by BP petrol station, turn right to Latem, then take first road left, Guido Gezellestraat; at the next crossing keep right, then take Hooglatemweg, and then the first street on the right

Roos Volckaert's garden is small but full of delightful things to please the eye. It is laid out around three sides of an attractive cottage and shows the influence of designer Elisabeth Lestrieux, as well as Vita Sackville-West's white garden at Sissinghurst in Kent.

This is a well-used garden, an extension of the house with several pretty arbours adorned with roses such as *Rosa* 'Kiftsgate', *R.* 'Phyllis Bide', and *R.* 'Blush Noisette'. It is decorated in a distinctive Belgian fashion, with arrangements of fruit and vegetables.

Roos Volckaert organizes the open garden scheme in the attractive wooded area south of Ghent.

open: The Plant Palace: Easter to last Sun in Oct, Mon to Thu, Sat, Sun, and Public Holidays, 1–4pm; last Mon in Oct to Easter, Mon to Thu, 1–4pm; the Outdoor Collection: as above during the summer but closes in winter; park: all year, daily, 9am–6.30pm

Further information from:
Domein van Bouchout, 1860 Meise
Tel: (02) 269 3905

Nearby sights of interest:
Brussels.

18

Nationale Plantentuin van Belgie

Location: 12km (7½ miles) N of Brussels by the A12 motorway, Brussels/Boom/Antwerp and then exit Meise

In the Middle Ages the castle of Bouchout was a defensive fortress. It was transformed in the 17th century and again in the 19th century in the English style. King Leopold II acquired it in 1879 and his sister, Charlotte, distraught widow of the Emperor Maximilian of Mexico, lived there until her death in 1927. In 1938 the Government bought the château from the Belgian Royal Family and restored it completely. The park, together with the adjoining estate of Meise, is now the site of the National Botanic Garden.

The Plant Palace has 13 different houses devoted to the flora of Africa, subtropical and tropical America, Australia, and Asia, laid out as landscapes, with tall trees like acacias, eucalyptus, and palms providing a canopy over shrubs and support for exotic creepers. There are also two houses where tropical plants are grouped according to their use rather than their origin. The famous giant waterlilies, *Victoria amazonica* and *V. cruziana*, are found in the Victoria Greenhouse, along with the sacred lotus, rice, papyrus, and the water lettuce.

The outdoor collections consist of an area of woody plants, comprising a shrub and tree collection and a pinetum. The herbetum or collection of herbaceous plants and the garden of medicinal plants are within this area. For the keen plantsman, with limited time, the minimal opening hours are a distinct frustration as there is insufficient time to see the collections properly.

In the garden of medicinal plants, species are grouped according to their effect on the human body. Among the conifers are groups of different cultivars of the same species. The shrub collection contains many good-sized shrubs: aralias, eleagnus, hamamelis, magnolias, and roses are represented. In late summer it is worth looking out for hibiscus, hydrangeas, hypericums, *Vitex agnus-castus*, and the rare *Franklinia alatamaha*.

Gardeners will find the systematic garden of herbaceous plants of great interest. The species are divided into sub-families in a half-hexagon around the elegant cast-iron greenhouse designed by Alphonse Balat in 1853. Again, the limited opening time is annoying.

The English landscape park, with ponds, avenues, and clumps of forest trees, covers about three-quarters of the total site.

Giant waterlilies cover the surface of the tank in the Victoria Greenhouse. In the foreground is *Nymphaea gigantea* with crenate leaves.

open: Last Sun in May and every Sun in Jun, 11am–6pm; groups may visit weekdays by appointment only

Further information from:
M. van Halle
Moerasstraat 6, 8840
Oostnieuwkerke
Tel: (051) 205 740

Nearby sights of interest:
Kasteel Rumbeke.

Caltha palustris in the corner of the formal pool next to the courtyard.

19 *Oostnieuwkerke: The English Garden*

Location: W of Roeselare/Roulers, 30km (18½ miles) S of Bruges; in centre of village at traffic lights take road to Roeselare; then third on right, Vijverstraat, signed to La Fermette; follow this road past La Fermette and through fields for several kilometres; Moerasstraat is on the right and the garden is signed

A garden of geometric compartments adjoins an English-style country garden with a lake, wild garden, and island beds. It is a delightful mixture of the formal and informal. One of the boundaries is a tall straight hawthorn hedge, very regular, yet it is left unclipped in spring.

The entrance court has box-edged beds full of perennials. The chosen perennials are all white, but the scheme is constantly upset by self-sown invaders adding touches of pink and blue.

The formal garden contains geometric flowerbeds, a rose garden, a rectangular pool, and a "room" which houses a crowd of box balls in different sizes. On the other side of the canal is a woodland garden where a stand of alders provides shade for ferns, geraniums, hostas, and *Viola labrodorica*. In the island beds near this tiny grove are astrantias, the summer-flowering magnolia (*Magnolia* x *thompsoniana*), peonies including *Paeonia lactiflora* 'Jan Van Leeuwen', a strong white peony, and thalictrums.

An attractive terrace surrounded by pleached lime trees and with a small pool adjoins the house. Pots filled with luxuriant zantedeschias and urns overflowing with the tiny Mexican daisy, *Erigeron karvinskianus*, decorate the area.

open: All year, Sun, 12 noon to 6pm; guided tour at 2.30pm

Further information from:
Heymansweg 2,
3670 Neerglabbeek
Tel: (089) 810 890
Fax: (089) 810 899

20 *Orshof*

Location: NE of Hasselt and W of Maseik, near the Dutch border; from E314/A2 Brussels to Aachen/Aix take exit 31, Meeuwen/Gruitrode; continue along N76 to Meeuwen, then take road to Gruitrode, right; Orshof is signed

Orshof is an ensemble of traditional farmhouse and buildings set in a remote rural corner of Limburg. Not that it seems remote for Orshof seems to be full of activities: groups of children camping, students who work in the centre, business people at conferences, Dr Van Orshoven's therapy groups, and garden visitors. The different buildings that make up the complex are connected by elegant glass structures, the winter gardens.

The garden is full of interesting ideas. Bold foliage is the most noticeable feature of the planting in the first part that one sees: 2.5m (8ft) high *Macleaya cordata*, luxuriant ferns, glossy ivy, close-textured yew, and box.

Outside the dining room window there is a large pool and adjoining seating areas, separated from each other by rings of "Ballerina" apple trees and columnar nectarine trees.

In the greenhouse outside the doctor's study, *Passiflora* 'Kaiserin Eugenie' (syn. *P.* x *belotti*) with large, sweetly-scented pink, white, and blue flowers blooms from March to November in company with an enormous strelitzia. *Magnolia grandiflora* grows against the outside wall, as does a trained vine. Nearby are the blue borders: standard hibiscus emerge from tradescantia and caryopteris in August. Then the blue-flowering herbaceous plants and shrubs give way to romneya and white agapanthus as the border changes from blue to white to yellow. Arum lilies in pots and a silver-leaved pear are followed by yellow phlomis and primulas.

The first conservatory to be built at Orshof accommodates the fruiting passion flower, *Passiflora edulis*, pink oleanders, and myrtle. Outside this glasshouse is the pink garden where in late summer there are pink hydrangeas, polygonums, and Japanese anemones. There is another pool here with a magnificent clump of the giant-leaved gunnera, *Gunnera manicata*.

One of the specially designed winter gardens.

---

21 *St Pieter: Patricia van Roosmalen*

open: First and third weekends in Jun, 10am–5pm; also by appointment

Further information from:
St Pieter 24, 3621 Rekem (Lanaken)
Tel: (089) 714 692

Nearby sights of interest:
Maastricht (Netherlands).

Location: 12km (7½ miles) N of Maastricht, on the Dutch border directly E of Hasselt; from Maastricht follow signs to Maseik which will take you on to the N78 to Lanaken; from A2/E314 motorway Leuven/Louvain to Aachen/Aix take exit 13 at Maasmechelen, then direction Lanaken on N78; Rekem is about 4km (2½ miles); turn into village and then follow directions to Oude Rekem; St Pieter is on the right

Patricia van Roosmalen's garden, one of the best small gardens in Belgium, has been described as an English garden but two of its most fascinating features, the oldest and the newest, are not at all in the English tradition. Along the main axis of the garden, a procession of the conical form of the white spruce, *Picea glauca* var. *albertiana* 'Conica', accompany the path down to the arbour created 100 years ago from the cornelian cherry, *Cornus mas*, which used to be a common hedging plant in Limburg.

The newest feature, but undoubtedly not the last, is the tiny 13 x 7m (43 x 23ft) fruit garden which contains no fewer than

Picea glauca var. *albertiana* 'Conica'.

52 fruit trees. Apple and pear trees are trained as cordons and espaliers. Patricia van Roosmalen describes her new fruit garden as a tribute to this area of Limburg. The layout is very formal, like a monastic cloister. A pattern of low box hedges is planted with herbs and strawberries, mixed with fritillaries, *Scilla sibirica*, and tulips. The rest of the garden follows similar rules: symmetry and straight lines are combined with an elegant and subtle informality of planting.

Two tall swamp cypresses guard the entrance to the calm garden, where there is a "quiet" shrub border and at the other end three golden fastigiate elms, *Ulmus* x *hollandica* 'Wredei'. Along the front of the house, hydrangeas, wisteria, *Solanum crispum*, and *Clematis tangutica* 'Bill Mackenzie' mingle.

---

open: Mr and Mrs Lenaert's garden: last Sun in May and last Sun Jun, 10am–6pm; also by appointment

Further information from:
Claire Hertoghe's garden: de Roskam 7, 2970 Schilde
Tel and fax: (03) 383 4850
Mr and Mrs Lenaerts' garden: Epicealaan 2a, 2970 's-Gravenwezel (Schilde)
Tel: (03) 383 5774

Nearby sights of interest:
Kasteel van 's-Gravenwezel; in Middelheim Park (Middelheimlaan 61, 2020 Antwerpen; open Tue to Sun, 10am; Oct to Mar closes 5pm, Apr to Sep closes 7pm, May and Aug closes 8pm, Jun and Jul closes 9pm) there is a famous sculpture park and château, now a restaurant; Plantin-Moretus Museum; Antwerp Zoo; Diamond Museum; Museum Mayer van den Bergh, which houses paintings from the 14th to the 16th centuries; Cathedral of Our Lady; Royal Museum of the Arts; Port of Antwerp.

22 *Schilde: Claire Hertoghe and Mr and Mrs Lenaerts*

Location: From Antwerp ring take E313 Hasselt–Turnhout; take exit 18, to N12 direction Wijnegem to Schilde; Claire Hertoghe's garden: continue through Schilde, direction Turnhout, until large trading estate, turn left 250m (270yds) beyond DIY store into Waterstraat and then take second turning left; Mr and Mrs Lenaerts' garden: as above to Schilde then continue to traffic lights and then left, direction 's-Gravenwezel, after 1.5km (1 mile) turn right into Hoge Haar by the Chinese restaurant, Epicealaan is the first turning on the left and 2a is on the right

Claire Hertoghe has created an English country garden with curving, beautifully planted mixed borders. One border is in pinks and mauves. Roses and deutzias give body, and self-seeded pink and plum-coloured poppies and purple-leaved *Atriplex rubra* add deeper notes.

All the trees in the garden have been grown since Mrs Hertoghe moved here. Many of the trees, like some of the birches, are self-sown. At the bottom of the garden, underneath a large *Betula nigra* there are yellow wild azaleas and bluebells in spring. Under the willows on the boundary, astrantias, epimediums, and *Hydrangea arborescens* 'Annabelle' do well. In a newly shaded border (the trees grow each year and the borders are replanted as their "aspect" changes) *Hydrangea aspera* and hostas take the place of the earlier sun-lovers. In this area there an informal pond with an attractive planting around it of mainly variegated and yellow plants. This is a garden where nature and the gardener work in complete harmony, and the result is delightful.

Mr and Mrs Lenaerts' garden of surprises hidden by tall enclosing hedges is divided into three areas: the wild garden, a vegetable garden, and the garden of old roses. In the wild garden grasses flourish and so does the wild azalea that is found in this area. The vegetable garden has peonies and delphiniums for cutting, and salad vegetables in rows. The rose garden is formal in layout, with a central path, one cross axis, and a seat at the far end creating a small vista. On either side symmetrical beds, planted with shrub roses and standard roses, are enclosed by low hedges of clipped box. Day lilies, large alliums, heuchera, hostas, and lavender soften the formality, making this a romantic and enchanted spot.

 # *Scholteshof*

Location: Just W of Hasselt; from Antwerp–Liège/Luik motorway A13/E313 take exit 27 Diest and turn right at the end, at Kermt turn left opposite church and Scholteshof is signed; from A2/E314 Brussels to Aachen/Aix take exit 25, Diest, and then N2 to Hasselt to left, at Kermt, in 12km (7½ miles) turn right opposite church and Scholteshof is signed

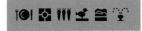

open: At all times

Further information from:
Kermtstraat 130, 3512
Hasselt-Stevoort
Tel: (011) 250 202
Fax: (011) 254 328

Nearby sights of interest:
Tongeren: Basilica of Our Lady.

The gardens, Giardini Scholteshof and the Four Seasons Vegetable and Fruit Garden, round this elegant and renowned hotel provide not only an attractive setting but also vegetables, fruit, and herbs used in the restaurant.

The garden has been developed in two stages. The pleasure garden is a handsome design of tall yew hedges, a beech *berceau*, ivy, and other evergreens. There are lawns, herbaceous borders, quiet enclosures, a pond, and a tiled gazebo. Tubs of box topiary, a maze, and box-edged beds of blue and white agapanthus are a contrast to the freer planting beside the pond and in the borders.

A long vine-covered pergola leads towards the orchard, herb, and vegetable gardens. Yew-edged beds in a regular pattern are found in one area and in another there is a pavilion covered with vines and clematis. There are rows of borage, rosemary, corn, tomatoes, sunflowers, lavender, beetroot, and courgettes. Billowing squares of *Melissa officinalis* 'Aurea', wild marjoram, different thymes, and velvety sages surround the rectangular pool in the herb garden.

There are a vineyard, pear walks, and areas of soft fruit, but the culinary interests of the owner spill into other parts of the garden too: there is a cutting garden with medlar and quince trees, a small enclosure which contains beds full of brilliant nasturtiums, and a circle of pleached pear trees with herbaceous borders around them.

Cool blue and white agapanthus fill box-edged beds around apple trees.

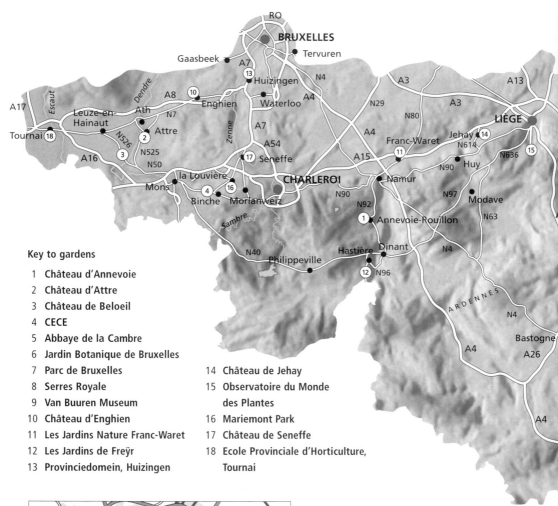

Key to gardens

1 **Château d'Annevoie**
2 **Château d'Attre**
3 **Château de Beloeil**
4 **CECE**
5 **Abbaye de la Cambre**
6 **Jardin Botanique de Bruxelles**
7 **Parc de Bruxelles**
8 **Serres Royale**
9 **Van Buuren Museum**
10 **Château d'Enghien**
11 **Les Jardins Nature Franc-Waret**
12 **Les Jardins de Freÿr**
13 **Provinciedomein, Huizingen**

14 **Château de Jehay**
15 **Observatoire du Monde des Plantes**
16 **Mariemont Park**
17 **Château de Seneffe**
18 **Ecole Provinciale d'Horticulture, Tournai**

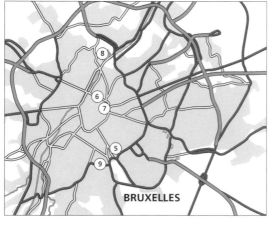

Key

═══ Motorways
═══ Principal trunk highways
③ Gardens
⬤ Major towns and cities
• Towns

Southern Belgium

and Brussels

Wallonia, which makes up southern Belgium, and Greater Brussels are two of Belgium's administrative regions. Unlike Flemish-speaking Flanders, in Wallonia the language spoken is French. The capital and its surrounding area, Greater Brussels, are bilingual and both Flemish and French are used equally.

In the wealthy province of Hainaut with rich fertile plains and rolling wheatfields there are several important historic gardens. The garden at Château d'Enghien (see pp.134–5) was the most important 17th-century garden in Belgium and after a long period of decline, has been undergoing extensive restoration. The classical French-style garden of Château de Beloeil (see pp.126–9), the wonderful arboretum of Mariemont Park (see p.138), the terraces of Château de Seneffe (see p.139) where the French Community has a gold and silver museum, and the mysterious "picturesque garden" of Château d'Attre (see p.125) are all well

Helxine is used to draw the eye to the statue in one of the corridors of the Serres Royale.

Thick yew hedges delineate the main axis at the Château de Franc-Waret.

The maze in the garden of the Van Buuren Museum in Brussels.

worth visiting. To the south, around Charleroi, rich coal seams have resulted in an unattractive area of mines and heavy industry.

Wallonia is divided geographically by the valley of the Sambre and the Meuse. On one side there are the mountainous Ardennes and on the other a landscape of farms, towns, and industry. Sandstone foothills rise to deeply scored, dramatic limestone scenery. Areas of Namur, Liège, and Luxembourg are remarkable for some of the wildest countryside in Europe with waterfalls, underground grottoes, and rivers cutting through steep gorges. This is not an area rich in cultivated gardens, although there are two fine historic gardens: Château d'Annevoie (see p.124), in the hills of south Namur, with Italian water features as well as French and English influences, and Les Jardins de Freÿr (see pp.135–6), with a formal garden of box parterres dating from the 18th century on the west bank of the Meuse south of Dinant.

The chapel of the Abbaye de la Cambre in Brussels is reflected in the adjacent pool.

To the south east of Brussels are fine woods which were once royal hunting grounds. Easily accessible by public transport from the city centre are the arboretum and park at Tervuren, the forest of Soignies and neighbouring La Hulpe, and the Domain of Bouchout at Meise (see p.114). The metropolis itself has many old squares and parks such as the historic and very formal Parc de Bruxelles (see p.132), dating from the 18th century, and the late 19th-century Parc Cinquantenaire/Jubelpark. Particularly exciting is the 20th-century garden attached to the Van Buuren Museum (see p.134) with its Art Deco furnishings and fine paintings. The Grote Markt or Grand' Place in the centre of Brussels is the scene of daily flower markets and every second August, is carpeted completely with flowers. Every spring the King of Belgium opens the enormous Serres Royale at the Royal Palace of Laeken to the public (see pp.132–3). There are private gardens open to members of the Belgian Garden Scheme and for a long stay, membership gives access to many well-designed and beautifully planted gardens.

The orange trees at Les Jardins de Freÿr are 300 years old.

 # *Château d'Annevoie*

open: 1 Apr to 1 Nov, daily, 9.30am–6.30pm; guided tours by request

open: 1 Apr to 1 Nov, Sat and Sun, 10am–5.30pm

Further information from:
Les Jardins d'Annevoie, 47 Rue des Jardins, 5181 Annevoie
Tel: (082) 611 555
Fax: (082) 614 747

Nearby sights of interest:
Namur: Citadelle, Musée de Groesbeeck de Croix; Abbaye de Floreffe.

Location: 17km (10½ miles) S of Namur; take the N92 towards Dinant; Annevoie-Jardines is signed right

Annevoie is situated in the wooded hills above the Meuse Valley. The hilly site and abundance of water persuaded Charles-Alexis de Montpellier to create gardens here that would rival those of the Villa d'Este in Italy.

The gardens were constructed between 1758 and 1778 and were much influenced by Charles-Alexis' travels in Italy, France, and England. All the fountains and cascades work from the natural pressure of the water, much of it stored in the Grand Canal above the garden, and jets of water over 6m (20ft) high shoot permanently into the air.

The Italian-style water sideboard, Le Buffet, dates from 1760 and was one of the earliest features to be constructed. Small jets in a symmetrical pattern emerge from a terraced grass slope and then cascade into a narrow rill.

Behind the château past columnar beeches are a series of *allées*, bordered by tall hornbeam hedges. The *grande allée* is bright with beds of snapdragons and scarlet salvias, and contains four *trompe l'oeil* statues of the four seasons: two-dimensional representations like cardboard cut-outs but surprisingly effective. A pond with a crown of jets is known as the "artichoke". A hornbeam tunnel-arbour turns to a right angle at a fountain jet which emerges from a mossy rock. This is called the Fountain of Love and is a place for making wishes.

Water takes many different forms in these magnificent gardens.

In the English style is the Rocher de Neptune, a picturesque if gloomy grotto in which the figure of Neptune sits beside one of the four sources of water which emerges here.

High on the hill above the castle is the Grand Canal. Rumour has it that if you walk the length of the canal, presumably wading through the water, you are one year younger at the end.

The garden has many fine trees which create patterns of light and shade, and soften the formal designs. The noise and sparkle of the water create a continuous sense of refreshment. Unless you are very gregarious it is best to visit outside high season although unlike many gardens, it remains a delight even on a hot August day.

² *Château d'Attre*

Location: 40km (25 miles) SW of Brussels; take A8 Brussels to Tournai and then exit 29, Ghislenghien, and follow signs to Attre; from Ath take the N56 to Mons, after 6km (3¾ miles) take left turn to Attre and follow signs to Château, which is on the edge of the village on road to Chièvre

The present château was completed in 1752 by the Count of Gomegnies to replace an earlier building. In front all is classical in appearance, with conical yews planted on each side of the central *tapis vert* and flowery motif in box near the château. There is a vista to the garden entrance, where Italian marble columns stand on either side of a small bridge. The axis continues across the road where there are two more columns. This design dates from 1913 and replaced the original *cour d'honneur*.

Behind the château the mood alters as the garden changes from reflecting order and reason to encompassing the romantic and irrational. A landscape park in the picturesque style, unique in Belgium, was laid out in the 1780s.

Set in a landscape of carefully made dramatic scenery and wild vegetation are five *fabriques* which add to the "picturesque" effect. Le Pilori is a relic of pre-Revolutionary times where those condemned for bigamy, lying, or prostitution would be pelted with rubbish by their fellows. Further along are the ruins of a 10th-century Norman keep. The third feature is a 19th-century Swiss Chalet set on a small mound.

The "picturesque garden" was designed to inspire awe, pity, and terror in the visitor. Attre today certainly generates an amount of anxiety. Even the Swiss Chalet, originally designed to create a lighter mood, is ominous. Scrambling up Le Rocher, the garden's most famous feature, is enough to set the visitor quite on edge. Le Rocher is an enormous artificial rock, 24m (79ft) high with a tower on top. In front of it there is a dramatic drop down to a hollow with more rocks and mysterious entrances leading to the labyrinth underneath the mound. If the feelings of awe and terror generated by just looking at the openings are not sufficient, it is apparently possible to enter the grottoes underneath the mound and pass from one side to the other. A pleasanter thing is to follow the path through the woods and come out by the fourth *fabrique*, the bath pavilion.

The fifth feature is Le Colombier, the dovecot or pigeon loft. This dates from the 17th century and can house 3,600 pigeons.

open: Easter to 31 Oct, Sat, Sun, and public holidays, 10am to 12 noon and 2–6pm; Jul and Aug, daily except Wed, same hours

Further information from:
Avenue du Château 8,
7941 Attre (Brugelette)
Tel: (068) 454 460

Nearby sights of interest:
Château de Louvignies; Parc Paradisio (7940 Cambron-Casteau; tel: (068) 454 653, fax: (068) 455 559; open Apr to 8 Nov, daily, 10am–6pm) is worth visiting for its magnificent 18th-century stairway and equally splendid row of massive, ancient plane trees.

This tower was built as a picturesque ruin.

Château de Beloeil

Location: SW of Brussels, 10km (6¼ miles) SE of Leuze

open: Apr to Sep, daily, 10am–6pm

Further information from:
rue du Château, B7970 Beloeil
Tel: (069) 689 426
Fax: (069) 688 782

Nearby sights of interest:
Château de Cambron-Casteau
(Parc Paradisio, see p.125).

Beloeil is Belgium's finest classical garden. The estate has been the seat of the Ligne family since the 11th century. The present château is a copy of that originally constructed in 1538 (and embellished in the Renaissance style in the 17th century) which was destroyed by fire in 1900. The magnificent gardens were laid out in the grand manner in the 18th century by Prince Claude-Lamoral II de Ligne with the probable assistance of French architect, Jean-Baptiste Bergé.

All parts of the original design are on a monumental scale: there is a lake 457m (1,500ft) long with a statue of Neptune at the far end. This is the first part of the splendid perspective from the château which extended for two miles beyond the gardens.

On either side of the lake are a series of enclosed gardens.

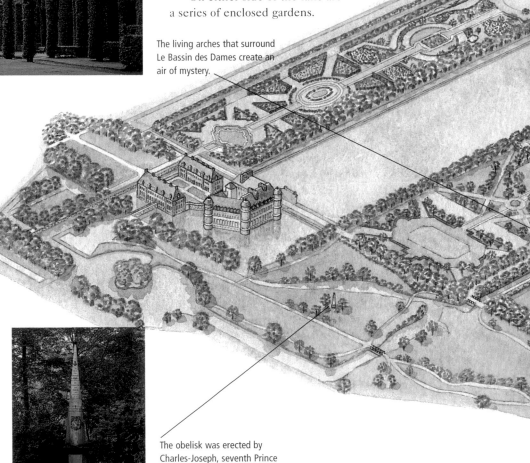

The living arches that surround
Le Bassin des Dames create an
air of mystery.

The obelisk was erected by
Charles-Joseph, seventh Prince
de Ligne in memory of his son.

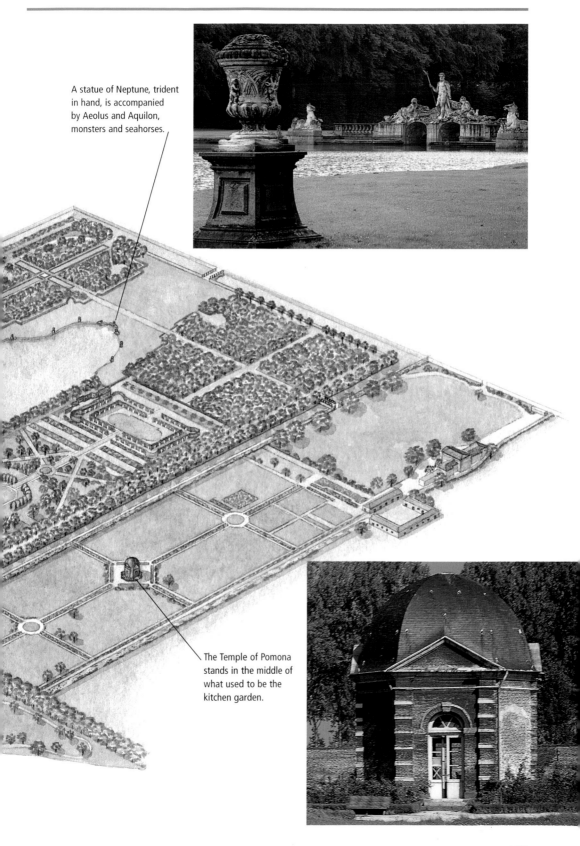

A statue of Neptune, trident in hand, is accompanied by Aeolus and Aquilon, monsters and seahorses.

The Temple of Pomona stands in the middle of what used to be the kitchen garden.

On the left, the first enclosure known as *le bassin vert* or the *boulingrin* once included a pool but is now simply a low mound of grass with gravel. Then comes the rose garden, which used to be filled with Bengal roses. Today the roses are red *Rosa* 'Dames de Coeur' and yellow *R*. 'Madame Meilland'. In the next enclosure, there is a children's playground and a goldfish pond in the centre of a newly planted *berceau* and hornbeams. The pond is full of weed and seems rather neglected. The oval pool which follows is surrounded by unclipped hornbeams.

Bordering the enclosures on this side is the long path known as the Dean's Lane, with hedges 6m (20ft) high. Between this lane and the hedges is a narrow stream, called Love's Rill, Rieu d'Amour, the creation of Prince Charles-Joseph de Ligne. Prince Charles-Joseph inherited Beloeil in 1766 and although entirely appreciative of its classical French style, was not immune to the fashions of the time and introduced several of the naturalistic features of the English landscape style. This winding rill and the narrow path that accompanies it was the first introduction. An English garden with a Temple to Morpheus and a copy of the ruined temple to the Sibyl at Tivoli were laid out with the help of François-Alexandre Bélanger, the French architect who built the Pavillon and gardens at Bagatelle in Paris. It is now referred to as the deer park and is not open to the public.

As a result of his works at Beloeil the prince became known as a designer and was asked for his advice about other gardens. He is believed to have suggested the idea of the Temple of Love in Marie-Antoinette's garden at Petit Trianon. However, in 1794 all idea of further work at Beloeil ended. The victory of the

Pierced yew hedges are reflected in the still pool.

French Revolutionary army at Fleurus forced the prince into exile. He went to Vienna and lived there in relative poverty as his estates, including Beloeil, were confiscated.

In 1804 Napoleon restored the estate to Ligne's second son (his first, Charles, had been killed while fighting the revolutionaries in France and there is a memorial to him, an obelisk which still stands, in the private garden at Beloeil). Charles-Joseph was never to return to Beloeil and although his circumstances did improve he was never able to think of the garden he had loved without a sigh.

The final section to the east of the lake is Les Miroirs, which is made up of four rectangular pools reflecting the sky and surrounding trees. A boundary canal acts as a ha-ha between the garden and the road. The curved end of the lake is decorated with urns on pedestals and a fine statue of Neptune flanked by reclining figures and lively horses.

Through the *quincunx* of copper beeches on the west side you can just see the 19th-century orangery. There is an avenue of oak trees alongside a series of *bosquets*. In the Cloister double hedges of hornbeam enclose a rectangular pool. The Ladies' Pool, Le Bassin des Dames, is surrounded by recently replanted hornbeam tunnels. There is a cross axis here from one side of the lake to the domed slate-roofed Temple of Pomona in the *potager*. This is one of the few cross axes with a focal point but it is spoiled by the intrusion of an ugly seat, an even uglier wastepaper basket, and a manhole cover. The final compartment is known as the Ice Pool, and here you will find a reflecting pool surrounded by an arbour.

The English garden is also known as the deer park.

The Temple of Morpheus is at the far end of the deer park. Double columns alternate with bays decorated with sculptured garlands.

Bray: CECE

open: All year but best time to visit is from Oct to May, Fri and Sat, 9am to 12 noon and 1.30–6pm; guided visits on the first Sun of month from Mar to Jun and Aug to Nov, telephone for a reservation

Further information from:
Avenue Léopold III, 12,
7130 Bray (Binche)
Tel: (064) 338 215
Fax: (064) 369 462

Nearby sights of interest:
Binche (Vieille ville); Château d'Havré (in ruins).

Patterns and colours of foliage are important at CECE.

Location: On the N90 midway between Mons and Charleroi; 3km (2 miles) outside Binche, direction Bray and Mons, turn right on to N27; CECE is on left, just before trading estate of Les Péronnes

This is a collector's garden attached to a specialist nursery, but there is much to interest and inspire the ordinary gardener. In particular there are many ideas for achieving year-round colour and grouping plants. Monsieur Benôit Choteau, who, with his wife, runs the nursery and the garden, is a true plantsman and the garden is full of rare trees, as well as common plants.

Immediately by the gate there is a group of *Prunus autumnalis*, witch hazels, and hellebores to attract visitors in the winter. To the left is the ornamental garden with colour-themed island beds. Equal attention is paid to the changing colours of the foliage of trees as to the flower colour of the herbaceous plants. A pieris is combined with a white rose from the Belgian grower, Louis Lens. Heathers in red, pink, and purple are grown with trees which enhance them: *Carpinus* x *schuschaensis* has striking red new foliage. *Cercis canadensis* 'Forest Pansy' is a rich purple colour, particularly exciting when the sun shines through the leaves.

There are more than 100 prunus cultivars, acers, beeches, chestnuts, hydrangeas, lilacs, magnolias, oaks, and peonies. *Acer palmatum* cultivars are particularly well represented in the garden, the new arboretum, and the nursery. The leaves are colourful all year, giving brilliant reds, dark reds, yellows, and green.

In the nursery beds there is a wonderful collection of oaks (as well as youthful versions of all the trees in the garden) which is a revelation to the non-specialist. As the trees are small it is possible to examine the different species and cultivars closely. *Quercus alba* has small rose-pink shoots and leaves in the spring, *Q. imbricaria* has dark glossy green leaves without any lobes, *Q. mongolica* has very large teeth on its leaves, and *Q. aegilops* (syn. *Q. macrolepis*) 'Hemelrijk' has bristle-tipped teeth to the leaves.

5 *Bruxelles: Abbaye de la Cambre*

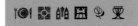

open: At all times

Location: Avenue Louise/Louizalaan; take tram 93 or 94 to stop Legrand and walk back towards the war memorial; cross to the right at Avenue Louise

Further information from:
Avenue E Duray – Avenue de Mot, 1000 Bruxelles

Nearby sights of interest:
Bois de la Cambre/Kameren Bos; Grand' Place/Grote Markt; Hotel de Ville/Stadhuis; Manneken Pis; Musée Royaux des Beaux-Arts de Belgique; Atomium; Galeries St Hubert.

The Abbey was founded in 1201. It was damaged by the Spanish in 1581 and in 1599 Albert and Isabella stayed there before they entered Brussels as regents for Philip of Spain. The gardens were terraced in the early 18th century when the fine *cour d'honneur* was planned. After the Revolution the Abbey was suppressed and the buildings became a cotton factory and later, a military school. Wounded from the Battle of Waterloo were cared for here in 1815 and it became a German hospital during World War II.

The entrance court is flanked by *pavillons d'angle* and the outbuildings in a semicircle. The garden was rescued from neglect and restored by Jules Buyssens in 1930. There are five different levels to the site, which is full of unexpected vistas.

6 *Bruxelles: Jardin Botanique de Bruxelles*

open: All year, daily

Location: Opposite end of Rue Royale/Konigstraat from the Royal Palace; metro: Botanique/Kruidtuin

Further information from:
Rue Royale/Konigstraat, 1030 Saint-Josse, Bruxelles

Nearby sights of interest:
Centre Belge de la Bande dessinée.

The former botanic garden dates from 1826. In 1939 the plant collections were moved to Meise. Now the elegant neoclassical glasshouses, 130m (426ft) long, are the cultural centre of the French-speaking community in Belgium and the gardens are open to all. Immediately in front of the domed central rotunda is a series of steps and terraces overlooking clipped box parterres. At each side of the parterres there are triangular beds edged with yew and filled with shrubs that billow out from their contrasting edging. These beds were designed by the landscape architect René Pechère in 1958. There is a large central pool with lively fountains which add sparkle and movement to the scene.

Many fine trees remain from the early days, including a *Diospyros virginiana*, the persimmon, *Celtis tournefortii*, *Acer trautvetteri*, and a large specimen of *Eucommia ulmoides*. To the north-west is an area of modern landscaping, planted with grasses and with a piece of contemporary sculpture as a focal point.

Beyond the Boulevard St Lazare the park continues down to a lake. There are sitting areas here secluded by hornbeam buttresses, a rose garden, and a layout of paths and shrubs.

The elegant neoclassical glasshouse dates from the 19th century.

open: At all times

Further information from:
Rue Royale/Koningstraat,
1000 Bruxelles

Nearby sights of interest:
Musées d'Arts Ancien
Moderne/Museum voor Oude
en Moderne Kunsten; Grand'
Place/Grote Markt; Palais
Royal/Koninklijk Paleis; Palais
de Beaux-Arts/Paleis voor
Schone Kunsten.

**Formal vistas reign supreme
in the Royal Park of Brussels.**

7 *Bruxelles: Parc de Bruxelles*

Location: Centre of Brussels behind the Central Station and between Parliament
Building and the Royal Palace; metro: Parc/Park

The formal lines of trees and the broad paths are reminiscent of
sections of the Tuileries in Paris. Parc de Bruxelles was the last
great formal park to be created in Belgium in the 18th century. It
was designed and laid out in the French style between 1774 and
1783 by Barnabé Guimard. Three straight *allées* radiate from a
large circular *bassin* and fountain surrounded by ivy and busts
of Roman emperors. The central path was designed with a
perspective view beyond the park, which now ends at the Royal
Palace in one direction and the Parliament Building in the other.
There are two cross *allées* and a hornbeam-edged walk all round
the park. In between these straight paths edged with formal rows
of trees are small *bosquets*.

Also in central Brussels, in front of the Royal Palace there
are some pleasantly informal parterres of rounded box, hollies,
euonymus, laurel, and yew. Further down the Rue de la
Regence/Regentschapstraat in the direction of the Palais de
Justice is the Petit Sablon/Klein Zavel. This garden, designed by
Beyaert in 1875, is surrounded by lime trees, ivy, and 48 pillars
on which small figures represent the different professions of
Brussels. Busts of Belgian worthies may be found in ivy-covered
arbours. The Counts of Egmont and Hoorn, who were beheaded
in the 16th century for leading an uprising against the Duke of
Alba, are commemorated by statues and a fountain.

---

open: Two weeks end of
Apr, beginning of May; Belgian
Tourist Office will advise opening
hours and days (including
some evenings)

Further information from:
Avenue du Parc Royal,
1020 Bruxelles

Nearby sights of interest:
Anderlecht: Maison d'Erasme;
Atomium; Parc de Laeken/Park van
Laeken; Tour Japonaise/Japanse
Toren; Pavillon Chinois/Chinois
Paviljoen.

8 *Bruxelles: Serres Royale*

Location: Take tram 23 and descend at Araucaria; walk past the Japanese
tower and bear left

The history of the Serres Royale at Laeken begins with the
Orangery. This classical building was built c1817/18 for William
I. By 1859 there was also a circular hot house with a crown on top
where the famous waterlily, *Victoria amazonica*, grew. It was not
until Leopold II's coronation in 1865 that the glasshouses were
extended to the 2ha (5 acres) they cover today. Before succeeding
to the throne, Leopold had travelled widely in north Africa,
India, and China where he had seen tropical flora growing in the
wild. He also virtually owned the Belgian Congo and it is from
the vast fortune that this made him that he was able to finance
his grand projects, including these glasshouses and the Royal
Museum of Central Africa at Tervuren.

Most of the buildings are curvilinear; the ironwork is painted a soft mint green and is decorated with flowing curves and circular motifs resembling the stems and flowers of plants. At intervals there are views into adjoining houses where fuchsias droop down from the roof and rows of perfect hydrangeas in glazed pots epitomize the 19th-century Winter Garden at its finest. The glasshouses are not planted to resemble tropical forests but to display a magnificent and immaculately maintained collection of tender and tropical plants: a superb spectacle.

The long glazed corridors between the glasshouses are lined with climbing geraniums and trained fuchsias with gnarled stems like old trees. One narrow corridor suddenly opens into a house full of massed, banked azaleas in glowing colours and then descends into a mirrored grotto, planted with stag's horn ferns. The next house, the Embarcadère, is decorated with enormous lace-cap hydrangeas and the following area contains immense ceramic urns on columns overflowing with the glorious Rose Grape, *Medinilla magnifica*. From here the route leads into the Congo House, where crotons, philodendrons, schizanthus, and cymbidiums grow in the lighter areas. The next spectacular sight is an avenue of tree ferns, including the delicious *Cibotium regale*, beautifully underplanted with nephrolepis and daisies.

The penultimate house is the circular Winter Garden, built in 1876. It is 34m (111ft) high and 68m (222ft) across, with a three-tiered glass dome. Round the sides there are clivias, cycads, justicia, and begonias growing in pockets in a fake rock wall, while the centre is a grove of tall palm trees. The last room is the Orangery, where mature rhododendrons, camellias, *Pittosporum tobira*, orange trees, and even a podocarpus are to be seen growing in massive *caisses de Versailles*.

Climbing pelargoniums, trained fuchsias, and palm trees line the mile-long glazed corridors of the Serres Royale.

open: All year, daily, 1–5pm; closes between Christmas and New Year

Further information from:
Rue L Errera 41, 1180 Uccle
Tel: (02) 343 4851

Nearby sights of interest:
Bois de la Cambre/Kameren Bos.

An aerial view of the maze.

9 *Bruxelles: Van Buuren Museum*

Location: In Uccle, near the Bois de la Cambre; trams 90 and 23, stop Winston Churchill, and buses 60 and 38

This interesting and unusual garden comprises an Art Deco-style rose garden dating from 1924, a garden in the English landscape style, a large rose garden, a maze, and the Jardin du Coeur.

The garden complements the house, now a museum. The English-style landscape garden is laid out around a large lawn and contains several exotic trees from Japan, including a catalpa, *Poncirus trifoliata*, the bitter orange, and *Pinus mugo*. The mixture of styles in the house is echoed in the garden. Modern art is reflected in the use of minerals.

The large rose garden contains roses such as *Rosa* 'Madame Meilland' and *R.* 'Queen Elizabeth'. Lower down an old tennis court has been transformed into a *boulingrin*. The maze is made up of 300 yews, creating seven green rooms. In the Jardin du Coeur a large heart, made up of twelve smaller hearts, was planted in memory of David van Buuren, the husband of Alice van Burren, who had died 15 years earlier.

---

open: Easter to 30 Sep, daily, 1–8pm; 1 Oct to Easter, Sat and Sun, 1–6pm

Further information from:
Place Pierre Delannoy, 6, 7850 Enghien
Tel: (02) 395 8360
Fax: (02) 395 4484

Nearby sights of interest:
Château de Gaasbeek; Château de Beersel.

10 *Château d'Enghien*

Location: 30km (18¼ miles) SW of Brussels; take E19/42 Mons/Paris motorway then exit 16, Halle to A8/E429 Tournai motorway to exit 16, Enghien

The famous park of the Dukes of Arenberg is undergoing major restoration. Swathes of trees have been felled in the woods near the Temple of the Seven Stars. Work on the temple and the Baroque and Renaissance gardens began in 1998; a garden of old roses is planned to complement the garden of dahlias there already.

Prince Charles d'Arenberg purchased the estate at Enghien in 1606 and began to redesign the entrance gardens. He brought orange trees from Brussels, pines from Spain, and vines from Arenberg to the neglected hunting estate. The main work on the gardens, however, was undertaken by his sons.

The domain is approached through a triumphal arch, surmounted by statues of a horse and rider surrounded by slaves. Beyond the stable block and underground galleries on the right are rose pergolas and sweeping lawns. This is where the first gardens were laid out: a rectangular pond surrounded by orange trees, *parterres de broderie*, dwarf fruit trees, and a labyrinth with an arcaded temple in the centre.

The Chinese Pavilion and the Pavilion of Paintings are on the right in the direction of the 20th-century château. In front of the château is a sunken lawn and to the left is the woodland intersected with long avenues of beech and chestnut, which converge upon the Temple of Hercules. This heptagonal pavilion is set in a circular *miroir d'eau* which reflects the Ionic colonnade. The trees being felled are those between the *allées* which radiate from the pavilion. Each *allée* was bordered by trees of different species such as beech, oak, chestnut, and cherry and there were subdivisions made by radiating smaller paths and two concentric rings of circular paths, and in between there were tiny curved woods surrounded by thorn palissades. These had been overgrown and hopefully will be fully restored.

An attractive pavilion at the edge of the woods.

11 *Les Jardins Nature Franc-Waret*

Location: Take N80 from Namur in direction of Hannut, E411 and E42; after about 10km (6½ miles) take a left turn to Franc-Waret

The nature gardens are a recent development at Franc-Waret. The garden has been leased by young visionary horticulturists and is being developed as an education facility. The garden behind the moated castle has a formal layout around a central axis. There are two main terraces each divided into four and the first four rectangles of lawn are minimally decorated with clipped box balls. The second terrace is planted as part of the *jardin nature* and the four sections are now a vegetable garden, a rose garden, a giants' garden, and the treasure garden. Beyond the terrace are the very pretty cottage garden and the aromatic herb garden.

open: 1 Apr to 31 Oct, daily except Mon, 10am–6pm; castle: same months, Sat and Sun, 2–6pm

Further information from:
Rue du Village, 54,
5380 Fernelmont
Tel: (081) 833 332
Fax: (081) 833 749

Nearby sights of interest:
Namur (Citadelle); Château de Fernelmont

12 *Les Jardins de Freÿr*

Location: On the W bank of the River Meuse, S of Dinant; take N96 in direction of Givet, castle is on the right after about 6km (3¾ miles)

The building of the pink brick castle of Freÿr began in 1571 and continued for the following century. In the 18th century, however, the owners, the Beaufort-Spontins, were elevated to the peerage and the castle was adapted to reflect their new status. At the same time the gardens were laid out. In 1759 the garden was divided into three long terraces parallel to the river. In the following year, a cross axis was created. It was not until 1774–5, however, that this axis was given a focal point with the construction of a pavilion.

open: Guided tours of house and gardens, 1 Jul to 31 Aug, Sat, Sun, and Public Holidays, 2–6pm; special opening on request for groups

Further information from:
5540 Freÿr (Hastière)
Tel: (082) 222 200

Nearby sights of interest:
Citadelle de Dinant; Parc National de Furfooz; Abbaye de Floreffe.

The first terrace is in three sections: a parterre with four pools symmetrically arranged and an area of pleached limes forming stilted enclosures around a central pool. Next there are two long rectangular pools surrounded by ranks of orange trees in white *caisses de Versailles*. These trees are historic survivors, having come from the court of Stanislas Leczinsky at Nancy nearly 300 years ago. During the French Revolution the local mayor decided to offer the orange trees to the Convention, but Robespierre fell and 33 of the original 50 orange trees were saved. In the last war a special donation of coal offered to keep the pregnant granddaughter of the house warm, saved them again. The fuel was used to heat the orangeries at the end of this terrace.

The terraced gardens seen from the opposite side of the River Meuse.

The second terrace is a symmetrical pattern of eight ornate parterres of box arranged round a central oval pool. This pool is part of the perspective to the delightful pavilion known as the Frederic Saal, or Frederic's Hall. Between the second terrace and the pavilion is the upper garden. From the pavilion the cliff on the other side of the river provides a magnificent wild backcloth to the geometrical formality of the garden.

♨ open: All year, daily, 9am–8pm; closes 6pm in winter

Further information from:
Torleylaan 100, 1654 Huizingen
Tel: (02) 383 0020
Fax: (02) 380 8444

Nearby sights of interest:
Kasteel Gaasbeek; Kasteel Beersel.

🍁 13 *Huizingen: Provinciedomein*

Location: 15km (9¼ miles) S of Brussels; E19 from Brussels ring R0 to Halle/Mons and take Exit 15, Huizingen; follow signs to Dworp and Provinciedomein is on left

A mound with grotto and fallen columns suggests that there may have been an earlier garden of some importance. Any other features have been swamped by recreational facilities, tennis courts, and trampolines. Standards of horticulture and maintenance are high but respect for any historic landscape is totally absent.

The best feature is a huge rock garden planted with flowering shrubs and trees. These are underplanted with azaleas, berberis, cotoneaster, and roses for all-year colour. Beneath the shrubs there are daffodils, heathers, pansies, and tulips.

The garden for those with little or no sight is very strange. Paths are edged with mahonia and berberis. Raised beds are furnished with Braille labels. Unfortunately there are not always plants to go with them and what plants there are – geraniums and ligularia – have presumably been chosen only for the texture of their leaves. There are groups of *Corylus maxima* and mounds of cotoneaster. It seems almost deliberately contrary, as if only sighted people delighted in the sweet scents of daphne, or lilac.

Attractive woodland surrounds the developed areas.

14 *Château de Jehay*

Location: 18km (11¾ miles) SW of Liège; from N17 Huy–Liège turn left at Amay towards Tongres; from Aachen–Paris motorway E42, take exit 5, St Georges, and then direction Amay for 4km (2½ miles)

The castle at Jehay has been in the property of the van den Steen family since 1680 and the garden was designed by the current owner. The formal garden has a rising central axis with a water staircase of linked basins on each side. These are adorned with rather meretricious statues of female nudes. This axis climbs towards a gate on the horizon. There are many good specimen trees, the remains of an ancient lime avenue, and a fine ice-house.

open: 1 Jul to 31 Aug, Sat, Sun, and Public Holidays, 2–6pm

Further information from:
4540 Jehay-Amay
Tel: (085) 311 716

Nearby sights of interest:
Musée du Château des Comtes de Marchin, Modave; Liège: Cathédrale St Paul, Musée de la Vie Wallonne, Collégiale Notre Dame, Huy.

---

15 *Liège: Observatoire du Monde des Plantes*

Location: From the centre of Liège, take motorway to Ardennes; turn off at Embourg; Université de Liège, Sart Tilman, and later Observatoire du Mondes des Plantes is signed

The 200 sq m (2,150 sq ft) of glasshouses is a joint enterprise by the European fund for regional development and the University. The layout is exciting and attractive, as well as informative.

The tropical house is lush with mounds of selaginella, ferns, palms, bananas, and cycads. A large pond of tropical waterlilies includes *Nymphaea* 'American Beauty' and the sacred lotus *Nelumbo nucifera*. At the top of the house is a pool crammed with more tropical waterlilies and in the centre the spreading round leaves of the giant waterlily, *Victoria amazonica* (syn. *V. cruziana*), compete with *Pistia stratiotes*, the hairy-leaved water lettuce.

In the cool house there are plants from areas of the world which have a Mediterranean climate, such as California and Chile. The Mediterranean region proper is divided into Garrigue – planted with artemisia, *Dorycnium hirsutus*, *Glaucium flavum*, and sage – and the Maquis with its different flora of cistus, atriplex, and genista. Californian plants are divided into those from Chaparral and Forest, with *Maclura pomifera*, fremontodendron, *Sisyrinchium bellum* (syn. *S. idahoense*), and *Umbellularia californica*.

Among the desert plants there is a wonderful *Kalanchoe orgyalis* 'Baker' with furry brown leaves. There is a well-planted display of ferrocactus: mammillarias, the strong white springs of *Fouquiera splendens* and *Bergerocactus emoryi*, and opuntias. Even stranger are the curving giant caterpillar forms of *Echinocereus vididfloris* from Colorado, Texas, and New Mexico.

open: All year, Tue to Fri 9.30am–5pm, Sat, Sun, and Public Holidays 1–6pm; times may vary

Further information from:
Université de Liège, Sart-Tilman B77, Parking 77, B 4000 Liège
Tel: (04) 366 4270
Fax: (04) 366 4271

Nearby sights of interest:
Grottes de Remouchamps; Liège.

Waterlilies in the tropical house.

open: 1 Apr to 10 Sep, daily, 10am–6pm; May to Aug, Sun and Public Holidays, 10am–7pm; Feb, Mar, and Oct, daily, 10am–5pm; Nov to Jan, daily, 10am–4pm; museum: all year except 25 Dec and 1 Jan, daily except Mon unless a holiday, 10am–6pm

Further information from:
Musée Royal de Mariemont,
B7140 Morlanwelz
Tel: (064) 212 193
Fax: (064) 262 924

Nearby sights of interest:
Do not miss the Musée Royale itself; Strépy-Thieu; Canal du Centre; les acenseurs hydrauliques.

16 *Mariemont Park*

Location: On the outskirts of La Louvière E of Mons, W of Charleroi; from E19/A7 Brussels–Mons motorway take exit 20, Feluy, and then direction Thuin via N59; from E42 Paris–Liège motorway take exit 19, Manage, then direction Mariemont

Many historic gardens have had dramatic changes both of fortune and of style. None more so than Mariemont or Mary's Mount which was named after Mary of Hungary, the widowed sister of the Emperor Charles V. In the middle of the 16th century she was made provost of Binche and chose the site at Morlanwelz for a hunting lodge. She laid out extensive terraced gardens in the Italian style and planted them with French roses. After Mary's death the estate was half abandoned until the arrival in 1598 of Archduke Albert and his wife Isabella, daughter of Philip II of Spain. By the beginning of the 17th century the gardens had become quite Spanish in appearance. In 1668 Louis XIV of France appropriated the estate. Nearly 100 years later Charles of Lorraine transformed the gardens in the French classical style. None of these gardens survived the French Revolution.

In 1830 an industrialist Nicolas Warocqué bought part of the estate and it is to him and his designer, C A Petersen, that we owe the romantic English landscape park and the fine trees that we see at Mariemont today.

The grounds are a mixture of open lawns with clumps of trees and woodland traversed by paths bordered with berberis, philadelphus, and *Prunus lusitanicus*. In the glades there are groups of rhododendrons and clumps of bamboo. *Phyllostachys viridiglaucescens* is dramatic among copper beech and cedars.

A green arbour in one of the rare formal areas.

The most splendid trees are grown as specimens in the grass. A monumental *Acer pseudoplatanus* 'Atropurpureum' spreads its branches low across the lawn between the winter garden and the rosarium. Further along the path there are groups of silver birch and a *Magnolia liliflora* 'Nigra'. There are also good collections of walnuts and two species of the related carya, birches, and acers as well as 100 different conifers.

Adjacent to the museum is a border of shrubs and climbing plants and nearby is a row of chamaecyparis cultivars. In the circular rose garden there are 70 different rose varieties.

It is for the nearly 600 different tree species that Mariemont is particularly renowned and anyone interested in trees should not miss it.

Château de Seneffe

Location: S of Brussels and N of La Louvière; from A7/E19 motorway Brussels–Mons take exit 20, Fley, then direction Seneffe; from E42 Mons to Charleroi and Liège/Luik take exit 18 bis, Chapelle-lez-Herlaimont, direction Seneffe; the museum in signed and near town centre

The garden and museum of silverware are approached through a splendid arcaded *cour d'honneur*, with statues and urns alternating in a series of niches. This splendour was designed to echo the new social status and wealth of Count Julien Depestre, a banker, who had the château built between 1763 and 1768. As with so many other châteaux, the house was sold by the family who were ruined by the French Revolution.

To the right of the château is the Garden of the Three Terraces, a formal garden in modern style designed by René Pechère. The first court with a central circular pool is rather arid. It is surrounded by pierced hedges of hornbeam and rows of seats backed by yew. Buttresses of yew against the walls make spaces for old roses, lilac, and lavender on the second terrace, where there is a spare geometric box parterre. On each side hornbeam-enclosed rooms contain empty metal plinths for sculptures, or trees and an ivy ground cover.

From the other side of the formal garden you can walk into the surrounding English landscape park and see the exquisite Theatre, a classical building with a pillared and domed bay.

The 1780 orangery, possibly the largest in Belgium, is on the left-hand side of the museum.

open: Daily except Mon; Easter to 1 Nov, 10am–8pm; 2 Nov to Easter, 8am–4pm; closes in bad weather

Further information from:
Musée de l'Orfèvrerie de la Communauté Française, Rue L. Plasman, 6, B7180 Seneffe
Tel: (064) 556 913

Nearby sights of interest:
Le Roeulx (Parc); Château d'Ecaussinnes-Lalaing; Collégiale St Gertrude, Nivelles.

Geometric parterre on the second terrace.

Tournai: Ecole Provinciale d'Horticulture

Location: Western side of Tournai ring road; from motorways take exit 34 to Tournai, from Kortrijk/Courtrai (note Tournai is Doornik in Kortrijk) on N50, turn right on to ring which is the Boulevard Léopold; the school is on the right signed IPEF

The first feature of this demonstration garden is a rock garden laid out round a pool. There are several fine trees, including *Ailanthus altissima* and sweet chestnut. Behind the ornamental front areas, there is the fruit garden with a fascinating collection of pear and apple trees trained as low espaliers, double cordons, and fans against the brick walls.

In another section there are groups of conifers, showing all their variety of colour and habit. There are also shrub borders, demonstration beds of roses, and extensive greenhouses.

open: All year except from 5 Jul to 20 Aug, Mon to Fri, 8am–4pm

Further information from:
Boulevard Léopold 92 bis, 7500 Tournai
Tel: (069) 222 037
Fax: (069) 843 824

Nearby sights of interest:
Cathédrale Notre-Dame; Pont des Trous.

Glossary

allées (French) Pathway which is bordered on both sides with plants, either trees or hedges.

bassin (French) A small formal pool which is usually made of stone.

beeldentuin (Dutch) A sculpture garden.

begraafplaats (Dutch) A cemetery.

berceau (French) A shaded arbour, often with seating, which is enclosed with plants.

bos (Dutch) Wood.

bosquet (French) A formal grove, often with a decorative glade, in which statues or other ornaments may be placed.

boulingrin (French) From "bowling green", and refers to a sunken lawn.

broderies (French) Ornate parterres with flowing designs which imitate embroidery patterns.

buffet d'eau (French) A type of fountain, popular in 17th-century France, in the form of steps over which the water falls.

caisses de Versailles (French) Wooden planting boxes.

cour d'honneur (French) The principal courtyard.

doolhof (Dutch) A maze or labyrinth.

demi-lune (French) Half-moon shape.

fabriques (French) Useful term covering a variety of garden features and constructions, such as pavilions, obelisks, and rotundas.

grand allée (French)

heempark or heemtuin (Dutch) A park or garden planted with native plants particularly wild flowers and grasses. The heemtuin movement was started by J P Thijsse in 1925.

kruidentuin (Dutch) A herb garden.

kwekerij (Dutch) A nursery.

miroir d'eau (French) A large formal pool which is designed in such a way that it is reflective, usually of the château.

moestuin (Dutch) A kitchen garden.

mount (English) An artificial mound.

parc à l'anglaise (French) Informal landscape park with winding paths, serpentine streams, and clumps of trees.

parterre (French) A formal bedding with low hedges, often box, disposed in a regular way and often incorporating topiary, urns, or other decorative devices. A *parterre de broderie* (French) A particular form of parterre in which the shapes of the hedges are arranged in flowing patterns which imitate embroidery.

parterres de compartiment (French) A symmetrical parterre.

patte d'oie (French) Goose-foot, three radiating paths from a central point.

plate-bande (French) Two parallel box hedges with flowers in the centre. In the Netherlands the plants are often widely spaced, each plant regarded as an individual specimen. The narrow strips of earth between may also be planted with conical yews.

potager (French) Kitchen garden, usually formal or decorative.

prieel (Dutch) Arbour.

quincunx (Latin) A grove of five trees, planted with one at each corner and one in the middle.

stinzenflora (Dutch/Friesian) In Friesland and the northern Netherlands, a Stins is a small noble house. The knights who inhabited them travelled to the Middle East on the Crusades and returned with small flowering plants they had discovered and planted them round their houses. Bulbs and corms, like tulips, snowdrops, winter aconites, and anemones, in particular were easily carried back to northern Europe. Eventually these became known as *stinzenflora*.

tapis vert (French) Lawn.

theeschenkeri (Dutch) Tea-house.

treintaxi (Dutch) For six guilders extra you can book a seat in a taxi from the nearest rail station to your destination at the same time as you buy the rail ticket. Additional stations and areas covered by this service are listed in a small leaflet available from Netherlands Railways and tourist boards.

trompe l'oeil (French) A style of painting in which objects are depicted as three-dimensional; literally "deceive the eye".

tuin (Dutch) Garden.

vaste planten (Dutch) Herbaceous perennials.

verrier palmette (French) A fruit trained to resemble a goblet.

vijver (Dutch) Pond or lake.

wandelroute (Dutch) Footpath.

warren (Dutch) Rabbit warren or occasionally in the Netherlands, refers to a deer park.

Biographies

André, Edouard François (1840–1911) French landscape architect who designed a number of gardens throughout Europe.

Copijn, Henri (1842–1923) Garden and landscape designer most well known for his work at the gardens of Kasteel De Haar. During his most fruitful period, between 1880 and 1905, he was greatly influenced by van Gustav Meyer's *Lehrbuch der schönen Gartenkunst*. His father, Jan Copijn, set up a nursery which was taken over by Henri Copijn and exists to this day.

Cuypers, P J Gothic revival architect known for his work at Kasteel De Haar.

Huygens, Constantijn (1596–1687) Dutch diplomat-poet and secretary to the Prince of Orange. He was an amateur architect and landscape architect and an exponent of Dutch classicism. He was influenced by and worked under the guidance of Jacob van Campen.

Marot, Daniel (1661–1752) A French Huguenot artist who trained in Paris before emigrating to the Netherlands, after the Revolution of the Edict of Nantes in 1685, where he became designer to William III. Marot adapted the Louis XIV style of garden ornamentation to the Dutch classical canal garden, resulting in a Franco-Dutch style. He collaborated with Jacob Roman on the ornamentation of the gardens at Paleis Het Loo, and his work may also be seen at Kasteel Twickel and at Kasteel Rosendael.

Michael, Johan Georg One of the first landscape designers of the Netherlands. At Beeckestijn (1772) he built a gothic temple and a hermitage, and he also worked on the gardens at Kasteel Twickel.

Petzold, C E A (1815–1891) German landscape designer, he was Director of Gardening at Ettersburg, near Weimar, from 1844. He did a considerable amount of work in the Netherlands and many of his garden plans were executed under the leadship of Leonard Springer. In 1888 Petzold was responsible for the partial reorganisation of the famous Clingendael in the Hague.

Poortman, Hugo A C (1858–1953) He studied architecture in Paris in his early twenties under Edouard André, who strongly influenced his style of garden architecture. Together with André, he went on a botanical expedition to Ecuador and Peru and brought back many exotic plants. He designed the parterres in front of the orangery at Kasteel Twickel.

Posth, J P In 1804 he landscaped Zypendaal Park, which was later reorganised by Petzold, under the request of van baron Brantsen.

Roman, Jacob (1640–1716) Dutch sculptor and architect to William III, who supervised the construction of the palace and the gardens of Het Loo.

Ruys, Mien (1904–) Dutch landscape architect who is regarded as one of the key figures in the development of the modern garden in the Netherlands. Her first designs were for country-house gardens, but her work expanded to include garden and landscape design for housing estates, industrial complexes, and offices.

Springer, Leonard A (1855–1940) A key figure in the development of park and garden design in the Netherlands, who is known for the introduction of the mixed-style design for small country-house gardens.

Thijsse, J P A Biologist and teacher who began the ecological approach to landscaping in the 1920s. He feared that the rapid expansion of towns and industries would destroy the natural landscape of the Netherlands. Following a design by Leonard Springer in 1925 he and his gardener created the Thijsse's Hof, near Haarlem. Stimulated by the development of botanical geography and the science of plant ecology led to the concept of the *heempark* or *heemtuin*. The most notable is the J P Thijsse Park, near Amsterdam.

Zocher, Jan David the younger (1791–1870) A distinguished Dutch landscape architect of the 19th century. He created many romantic landscape parks and the first public park in the Netherlands, Vondel Park, was laid out by Zocher and completed in 1877. Among his best known works are Kasteel Twickel and Kasteel Rosendael.

Index

Photographic acknowledgements

Front jacket: Garden Picture Library/Marijke Heuff
Back jacket: Barbara Abbs (top and bottom); Garden Picture
Library/Marijke Heuff (middle)
Inside back flap: Jackie Anthony/Theo Abbs

Barbara Abbs 1, 7, 8, 9 top, 9 bottom, 13, 14, 15 top, 15 bottom, 16,
18, 19, 21, 23, 24, 25, 26, 28, 29, 35 top, 36, 37, 39, 41, 43 top, 43
bottom, 45, 48, 49, 50, 51, 52, 53, 54, 55 top left, 57 bottom, 58, 60,
63, 65, 66, 68, 69, 70, 71, 74 bottom, 74 top, 75 bottom, 77 bottom
left, 77 top, 79 bottom, 80, 83, 84, 85, 87, 88, 89, 90, 91, 93, 95, 96
bottom, 96 top, 98, 99, 103, 104, 105, 106, 112, 115, 116, 119, 121,
122 top, 123 top, 133, 136, 138, 139;

Piet Bekaert 10-11, 113; Green Service, Community of Beveren
101; Domein Bokrijk 102; Musée van Buuren 134; Centre d'Étude
et Création d'Espaces Verts /Benoit Choteau 130; Cees van Dam
44; Delft Cultuurtuin 82; Jean-Pierre Gabriel 97, 107, 110, 111 top,
111 bottom, 123 bottom, 132; Garden Picture Library/Henk
Dijkman 47, 55 top right, 55 bottom, 62, 76 bottom, 77 bottom
right, /Henk Dijkman/Marcel Malherbe 5, 75 top, 78, 118,
/Marijke Heuff 2-3, 17, 27, 30, 31, 38, 56, 57 top, 59, 64, 73, 81,
/Lamontagne 86, /Brigitte Thomas 122 bottom; Robert Harding
Picture Library/K Gillham 131; Irene Jansen 20; Kasteeltuinen
Arcen 76 top, 79 top; H C Koningen 42, 46; Marianne Majerus
124; Nederlands Openlucht Museum 61; Observatoire du Monde
des Plantes, Université de Liège 137; F Van Orshoven 117;
Albert de Raedt 100; Sophora vof 22; Patrick Taylor 125, 135;
Tegelen Botanische Tuin Jochum-Hof 92; Tijdsbleed nv/Bart
Cloet 128, 129 top, 129 bottom; Stichting Twickel 34 bottom,
34 top, 35 bottom; University of Utrecht Botanic Gardens 67;
Roos Volckaert 114